Empowerment of Women and Microfinance

P. Muthaiyan

SERIALS PUBLICATIONS
NEW DELHI (INDIA)

First Published - 2011

ISBN: 978-81-8387-457-1

Published by

SERIALS PUBLICATIONS
4830/24, Prahlad Street, Ansari Road
Darya Ganj, New Delhi-110002 (India)
Phone : 23245225 Fax : 91-11-23272135
E-mail: serials@sify.com

Contents

Preface

The volume presents a collection of thirteen research papers devoted to Indian economy and related economic developmental issues. These research papers are contributed by subject experts holding prestigious position in Indian Universities and educational institutions of great esteem and world status dealing with economics. These papers are extremely comprehensive containing relevant statistics, tables, and latest various economic theories. These papers are produced at such a juncture when the whole world is passing through economic crisis. The research papers present not only national economic phenomenon but also global economic scenario in connection with global financial crisis. The factual information and treatment of these research papers are eye opener and shows how the Indian economy is boldly facing this world recession and depression in economy.

These papers may be listed below: Economic Recession 2008: Is Global Economy gets cold when USA sneezes? , Economics of Alternative Sources of Energy, Economics of Health Insurance in India, Is India Facing a Recession or a Slowdown of Growth, Microfinance and Disaster Management: An institutional Approach., Genetic Analysis of Some Important Quantitative Traits Across: Two Environments in Linseed, Application of Integer Programming Model for Optimizing Design Facility Using Lean Manufacturing, Human Rights Violation in India: A View, Crops Production and Fertilizers consumption in Tamil Nadu, : An impact of technology Adoption, Globalization, Urbanization and Urban Environment: An Issue and Challenges. Women Employment in the Export Processing Zones in India: A Measure for Social Protection, Micro Credit and Empowerment of Women through Self-Help Groups: An Institutional Framework, Present Status of Commodity Derivatives Market in India: Regulation and Policy Issues.

A Arunachalam, who is Faculty Member and Head of Department of Economics, Cochin University, of Science and Technology, Kochin, discusses 'Economic Recession 2008, International Monetary Fund Report paints a grim picture of the global economy in 2009, IMF's Chief Economist expect the world economy to come to virtual halt' if the growth prognosis comes true. This showed decreasing industrial production, inflation, decreasing job opportunities, cost cutting, reducing purchasing power parity etc. The phenomenon has been expressed through various terms, as Global Meltdown, or Global Financial Crisis, World Economic Crisis, Global Turmoil and Global Recession etc. It has been discovered that during the period between late summer of 2005 and summer of 2006, the flourishing US Housing market blocked suddenly and eventually the markets started facing effects like falling prices, and reduction of sales volumes. Around the world Stock Markets have fallen, large financial institutions have collapsed and even the wealthiest nations have had to come up with rescue package to lent out their financial systems. The paper is an eye opener of all important events leading to global economic crisis. It fully explains what is financial crisis and economic recession including the recession of 1930 and its effects on Indian Economy. After explaining the phases of business cycle further illustrates history of recession at global level specially US economy during the recession period. Financial convulsions which has appeared in America is threatening the economic stability of the whole world. US Slowdown is always an bad news for the world. Therefore, if US sneezes, it has certain impacts on world economy. In this paper, a complete and comprehensive picture of recent recession in its right perspective is presented and the reader will not miss any such information which is essential for the study of the topic.

J Srinivasan, Reader in Economics at Pondicherry University Pondicherry, studies the very important topic of 'economics of health insurance in India'. The topic is gathering heat since health is at stake in this industrial age and medical expenditure is increasing day by day. From an economic perspectives insurance is a financial intermediation function by which individuals are exposed to a specified contingency. From a legal perspective insurance is an agreement between the insurer and who insures. The article examines the subject under heads like introduction, categories of life and health insurance-like group insurance, industrial insurance, ordinary insurance. Under Section-2, it studies economic basis for life and health insurance. Demand for life and health insurance, concept of human capital, economic theories of consumption, consumption theories and insurance, production of life and health insurance, insurance production process, Section-3 discusses human life value concept,

Section-4 deals with health insurance in India, while Section-5 concludes the topic. Health insurance in India finds a full treatment of topic. Health insurance is mostly neglected subject with our insurers in India. In the year 1993, LIC identified four major diseases as Cancer, Paralytic Stroke leading to disability, renal failures (both kidneys) and coronary artery diseases. It further discusses life insurance policies as Asha Deep I, Jeevan Asha II, Asha Deep II and premiums and period for insurance by the insurers. The paper also researches on current scenario and issues in Health insurance in India. Healthcare sector in India is fragmented between the Centre and the States. The Government of India was a par to the 1978 WHO Declaration (Alma Ata Declaration) and commitment of 'Health for all by 2000' but precious little as obtained by the target. It presents in tabular form the 'selected health coverage in India'- CGHS, Mediclaim, Unversal Health Insurance Scheme, ESI, Non-Government LIC, etc. It also examines Private health insurance in India. Although a number of private insurance companies have entered after liberalization of the insurance market after 2000, no significant change in health insurance has been observed either in terms of new health insurance product or in terms of the volume of business. The two health products namely Mediclaim for the general public and Jan Arogya for the poor, launched prior to the liberalization, have not shown any significant growth either in terms of volume of business or in the number of policies sold post-lilberalization. Details have been shown through statistics in tabular form. Health insurance business in India will continue to evolve. Health Insurance is also a good device under social Security measures.

R Kumar and K Sambasivam holding prestigious positions in Annamalai and Pondicherry Universities, have discussed a very important topic of the day viz. Microfinance and Disaster Management: an institutional approach. Some times back the concept of microfinance and disaster management have not taken birth. Microfinance is the provision of relevant and affordable financial services to the poor household that do not have access to the service offered by the traditional financial institutions. The micro prefix refers to the size of the financial transaction. The paper examines microfinance and disaster management, natural disaster, disaster mitigation and disaster management, economic coping mechanism of poor household, impact of natural disasters on microfinance, role of microfinance in disaster relief, post-disaster rehabilitation, disaster related financial products and services, loan measures, insurance measures. It is a comprehensive study of microfinance and disaster management.

S Vijayen of Annamalai University, Annamalainagar, examines in details the important issue of Human Rights Violation in India: A view. Human Rights are most discussed rights these days. Government of India have set up a forum for redressal of human rights violation by Constituting the National Human Rights Commission (NHRC) and provides for the setting of State Human Rights Commissions under the protection of Human Rights Act, 1993, The constitution of India has provisions and guarantee for safeguarding almost the entire gambit of civil and political rights. Directive Principles of State Policies further require the states to ensure the promotion and protection of social cultural and economic rights. A National Action Plan for the human rights education, adopted by the Government of India envisages promotion and awareness of human rights to all sections of society. Ministry of Home Affairs has taken various initiatives for the spread of Human Rights education. Such as Human Rights Courses have been introduced as a part of the training for the Border Security Force and the Central Reserve Police. The Government have fully cooperated with various human rights agencies functioning under United Nations. The article delineates custodial violence, trafficking in Women and Children, Human Rights Awareness, education and training. Human Rights violations being implemented on Dalits. Caste system in India is factor towards violence where dalits are being tortured and harassed and where human rights least cared for. It also discusses human rights violations against dalits in India, human rights violations against dalits children, Dalit women. Role of international Non-Governmental Organizations in the field of human rights is also detailed. Dalits have been considered the most depressed, downtrodden, exploited and the lease educated in Indian Society. Dalits experience the agony of untouchability very deeply in all walks of life. Social, economical, political until to-day. India's Caste System which is a four-layered Caste system has compelled them to perform the most inhuman jobs in the society.

A Abdul Raheem and K Sambasivam have in their article entitled, 'Women Employment in the Export Processing Zones in India: A Measure for social Protection examine the details of the Export Processing Zone and Women employment in them. The process was most marked over the period 1990 to 1995, in the high exporting economies of East and South East Asia, where the share of female employment in the total employment in the EPZ and Export Oriented manufacturing industries typically exceeded 70%. Women workers are preferred by employers in export activities for various reasons. Since women workers have lower reservation wages. The idea of the EPZ-which is also known in other countries of Asia as a free Trade Zone, Special Economic Zone and so on, essentially to provide special incentives to exporters and to allow them to avoid many of the laws and physical and material constraints which supposedly inhibit export growth in the rest of the economy. In India, the first EPZ was established in 1960, which was one of earliest of all developed countries. At present there are seven EPZ operating within the country, while two more are planned. The largest are - Santa Cruz EPZ, Noida EPZ, and Madras EPZ. The numerial dominance of women workers is a characteristic feature of EPZ across the world. In both Santa Cruz EPZ and Madras EPZ women workers constitute 70-80% of the total workforce and average age of the women workers is estimated below thirty years in both the EPZ. But in Noida EPZ, which is only the exception where only 30-35% women workers are employed. The EPZ are also governed by labour laws of the country. The Bonus Law prescribes a minimum 8.33 % and maximum of 20%. The paper examines the EPZ in all its perspectives- social, legal , political, working conditions, administrative set up, measures for social protection of women workers. Social security programmes and welfare institutions being set up for the most vulnerable groups. Integrated Rural Development Programs is a addition to these measures which tried to provide basic assets to targeted rural beneficiary household and the employment schemes under various heads, public health program, public distribution system, social insurance etc.

Let me conclude that all these useful, information and comprehensive articles of subject experts of the field appended to this single volume presents a complete study on some of the economic issues of Indian Economy in proper and other related research papers to the Indian Economy at one place. The latest information furnished under these papers enable the students of economics and research scholars to equip themselves with the latest information on these issues. The volume will prove very useful for the all the concerned quarters. These articles in the form of a book is worth purchase for all the libraries, information centres specially the specialized libraries on Economics and related subjects.

International Journal of
RELIABILITY QUALITY AND OPERATIONS MANAGEMENT

IJROOM
Vol. 1 ■ Nos. 1-2 ■ Jan.-Dec. 2010

Economic Recession 2008: Is Global Economy Gets Cold When USA Sneezes?

P. ARUNACHALAM*

A recent IMF report paints a grim picture of the global economy in 2009. It forecasts economic growth around the world to fall to 0.5 per cent, its lowest in 60 years. This pessimistic view permeates IMF's latest update to its World Economic Outlook 2008. The IMF's chief economist expect the world economy to come to a 'virtual halt' if the growth prognosis comes true. In November last year, the WEO had predicted the world economy to grow by 2.2 per cent this year. So the most recent forecast is 1.7 per cent points lower than what the IMF had estimated as recently as four months ago. In fact economic news from every corner of the globe has been one never ending story of successive downward revisions of anticipated growth rates. In this research paper an attempt has been made to analyse various aspects of recession in 2008 and what would be its impact on the global economy?

The world seems not quite. Wherever you go people discuss about the US recession only. Economists, Politicians, Industrialists, environmentalists and the common man on the streets seem to have been horrified by the very thought of recession in India and that too due to US. Decreasing industrial production, inflation, decreasing job opportunities, cost cutting, reducing purchasing power parity, etc,. If one goes through past two years of Journals, magazines, government reports, medias both press and TV channels coming from different parts of the globe, one of the important items which occupy fifty per cent of the coverage is related to 'global meltdown', or 'global financial crisis', or 'world economic crisis', 'global turmoil' and "global recession".

* Faculty Member, Head (2004-07), Department of Applied Economics, Cochin University of Science and Technology, Kochi-22 (*E-mail: arunachalam14@yahoo.co.uk*)

Why it has attracted this much attention among these countries? And why it created a war like situation among 195 countries in the world? The reason is simply a housing problem that has brought the development of the entire world, particularly USA and European countries to a minimum level. The current economic situation in the world is very unpredictable and nobody knows the consequences of the current financial turmoil. In the respective of many economists the causes they perceive are different and there is no consensus about the causes of the current financial turmoil. However, majority of economists agree the financial crisis is unprecedented and it is a challenge to market economies. As well, they all agree the effect of this crisis is complex in nature and its unpredictability. The world financial crisis, the result of financial liberalization and an excess of global liquidity, has pushed the world into the recession. The global financial crisis, brewing for a while, really started to show its effects in the middle of 2007 and into 2008.

Joseph Stiglitz has stated that during the period between late summer of 2005 and summer of 2006, the flourishing U.S. housing market blocked suddenly and eventually the markets started facing effects like falling prices and reduction of sales volumes. The growing interest rates and home prices directly influence the housing market in U.S. A report from Barron's magazine reveals that the median price of new homes has dropped about 3% since January, 2006. The existing home inventories were 39% higher than they were one year ago and the sales were down by more than 10 per cent. It was also predicted that the national median price of housing will probably fall by about 30% in the coming years. The chief economist of NAR (National Association of Realtors), David Lereah predicts that the home prices would reduce by 5% nationally. The NAR also reported that National home sales and prices both dropped dramatically again in March 2007. In March 2006, the sales dropped by 13% to 482,000 from the peak of 554,000 and in July 2006, the national median price dropped about 6% to $217,000 from the peak of $230,200. Since 1989, the existing home sales in U.S. dropped abruptly and consequently the home market started suffering. According to a report by Commerce Department, the median prices for newly built homes in U.S. dropped by 10.9 per cent. A slowdown in US housing market impels the World Bank to lower the global economic growth rate. A worsening of the U.S. housing market could negatively affect the consumer confidence and at the same time will worsen the U.S. Economy and the economy of the rest of the world. As a consequence, the unemployment levels expected to stay low in the coming years. The Congressional Budget Office estimates an unemployment rate by 5.0% between 2006 and 2007 and between 2008 and 2011; the average annual unemployment rate will be 5.2 per cent. Low confidence levels could affect the consumer spending in an adverse manner and at the same time could negatively affect the residential construction.

Around the world stock markets have fallen, large financial institutions have collapsed or been bought out, and governments in even the wealthiest nations have had to come up with rescue packages to bail out their financial systems. On the one hand many people are concerned that those responsible for the financial problems are the ones being bailed out, while on the other hand, a global financial meltdown will affect the livelihoods of almost everyone in an increasingly inter-connected world.

In this book the author discusses some basic issues related to the problem, how it affects India and what are the bailout packages by the capitalist, communist and mixed economies in this world to stop this recession process.

Traditionally the basic and fundamental needs of human beings, based on their importance, are classified as 1. Food 2. Cloth and 3. Shelters. But Maslow's Hierarchy of Needs (1) has classified them into five 1. Physiological Needs, 2. Safety Needs 3. Social Needs, 4. Esteem Needs, 5. Self-Actualization. Whatever may be the classification, once a man's stomach is filled he thinks of getting good cloth and a nice place to rest that is a shelter. In 2005 an approximated 1 billon did not have suitable housing and 100 million were totally homeless. Out of total population in this world 6,749,391,759 billion. As many as 3.5 million people experience homelessness in a given year (1% of the entire U.S. population or 10% of its poor), and about 842,000 people in any given week (Wikipedia and Answers) (2). Of the 111 million households in the United Sates, about 76 million own their homes, and of these just over 50 million have a mortgage (Robert E. Hall and Susan E. Woodward, 2008) (3). According to the *National Coalition for the Homeless,* there are approximately 760,000 people who are homeless in the United States on any given night, 2 million have been homeless at some time during the year, and 12 million of the adult residents of the U.S.have been homeless at some point in their lives (4).

Pioneered by Dr. Sam Tsemberis, a faculty member of the Department of Psychiatry of the *New York University School of Medicine,* and the organization *Pathways to Housing* in *New York City* in the early 1990s, Housing First is premised on the notion that housing is a basic human right, and so should not be denied to anyone, Housing First is currently endorsed by the United States *Interagency Council on Homelessness* (USICH) as a "best practice" for governments and service-agencies to use in their fight to end homelessness in *America* Housing First programs currently operate throughout the United States in cities such as *Anchorage, Alaska; New York City; Denver, Colorado; San Francisco, California; Atlanta, Georgia; Chicago, Illinois; Quincy, Massachusetts; Philadelphia, Pennsylvania;* and *Seattle, Washington,* among many others, and are intended to be crucial aspects of communities' *10-Year Plans To End Chronic Homelessness* also advocated by USICH.

While there is no one agreed upon definition, one definition originally developed as part of the *McKinney-Vento Act* of 1987 *federal legislation,* describes a "homeless" person as being:

1. An individual who lacks a fixed, regular, and adequate nighttime residence; and an individual who has a primary nighttime residence that is—
   (i) A supervised publicly or privately operated shelter designed to provide temporary living accommodations (including welfare hotels, congregate shelters, and transitional housing for the mentally ill);
   (ii) An institution that provides a temporary residence for individuals intended to be institutionalized; or
   (iii) A public or private place not designed for, or ordinarily used as, a regular sleeping accommodation for human beings (5).

WHAT IS FINANCIAL CRISIS?

A financial crisis almost always involves the collapse of a country's currency, which loses much of its value against the dollar. This is why economists sometimes speak of currency crises as the generic expression covering all kinds of meltdowns. Exactly what else is involved in a crisis changes from country to country and also has tended to change over time. Sometimes the crisis comes with a default of the government, who finds itself unable to pay the now more expensive external debt. Other times, it is the private firms who cannot pay. In other instances, it is the banks that get into trouble, as their two major credit customers - the government and the corporations, are weakened, and the public, anticipating problems runs for the exits, precipitating a banking crisis.

A financial crisis has happened with regular intervals throughout the last century, it happens again in the year 2008, and probably will happen in the future in much the same way. There is no fundamental differences between such crises in our time and former crises, except perhaps that they occur faster, occur more frequently, but fortunately also heal faster.

An important cause of the crisis is over-optimistic companies and individuals during the foregoing period of economic growth. They tend to believe that the general growth will continue forever without interrupting periods of economic decline. They also tend to overestimate themselves and think they will be a winner in the competition against other companies or persons, not a looser, not an average performer, but the winner. This optimism, which is a general human property, makes all actors borrow massive amounts of capital and invest them in homes, luxury objects and expansion of their business. This expansive behaviour tends to accelerate for quite a long time until in meets the wall. Another cause are executives in banking companies tempted to lend out as much money as possible to the borrowers, regardless of the consequences for the bank and the borrowers, because this behaviour gives the executives an enormous short term personal gain.

The term financial crisis is applied broadly to a variety of situations in which some financial institutions or assets suddenly lose a large part of their value. In the 19th and early 20th centuries, many financial crises were associated with *banking panics,* and many *recessions* coincided with these panics. Other situations that are often called financial crises include *stock market crashes* and the bursting of other financial *bubbles, currency crisis,* and *sovereign defaults* (6).

Many economists have offered theories about how financial crises develop and how they could be prevented. There is little consensus, however, and financial crises are still a regular occurrence around the world (Wikipedia) (7).

If a bank lends ten dollars and charges a dollar interest, then the borrower must repay $10+1. No problem if the monetary system contained $100,000,000 of non-debt based money to begin with. The borrower can obtain an extra dollar somewhere from the pool of permanent money circulating in the economy to repay his loan. However, contrary to what most people think, when the bank "lends" the $10, it doesn't come out of the $100,000,000. It is "credit". The borrower's promise to repay (the signed loan document) is used to justify creating $10 of bank credit (borrower debt) in a bank account. That "credit" is indistinguishable from the permanent money, and so it is in effect money, too. This is what people mean when they say,

"Banks create money". It is true; they do. Now, temporarily there exists $100,000,010, and gradually as the loan is repaid, the amount reduces back down to $100,000,000, the credit is extinguished and only the permanent money remains once again. But, one dollar has changed hands from the non-financial world to the financial world. At the end of the loan period, there is $100,000,000 permanent money again, $99,999,999 + $1 paid in interest to the bank. Sounds pretty benign, eh? The problem is that the mathematics looks radically different when the modern fractional reserve banking system is examined. Without getting into all the gory mathematics, which in my experience most people cannot stomach without first downing a quart of express or Jack Daniels first, depending on their favorite vice, let it suffice to say that some permanent money exists in the system, but it is relatively insignificant. That bank "credit" money now makes up 97%-99% of all money and permanent money makes up maybe 1%-3% of all money. Let's say $75 trillion exists, and 2% is permanent money. That's $73.5 trillion dollars worth of bank credit, and $1.5 trillion of permanent money. I would be willing to bet there isn't that much permanent money, but it doesn't really matter. Close enough. People are paying interest on $73.5 trillion of bank credit. The credit created the principle, but not the interest. So, the people must fight over the $1.5 trillion of permanent money to get the interest needed to make payments on their loans. Let's just say the average interest rate of all loans is 5% per year. That's $3.675 trillion per year, out of $1.5 trillion of permanent money. It is not possible. So, what do the banks do? Lend more money, of course, so people can go deeper into debt but at least they can still make their loan payments. Does that sound like a pyramid scheme? Of course it does. That is why the pyramid is on the one dollar bill. It is one big inside joke. Once this system is in place, gradually indebtedness grows until bank credit displaces permanent money as the dominant form of money, and people and Government become permanently indebted to the banks. The banks own us individually and our Government, too it's like the first Great Depression, but it might be worse because the Fed thinks it has the solution this time. The first depression was caused by the inherent inability of the banking system to tolerate anything less than constant growth of the money supply. A slowing of the money supply caused the pyramid scheme to collapse. This time the Fed thinks the solution is - just create more credit money and the money supply will never drop. (8)

Ben Bernanke "As in all past crises, at the root of the problem is a loss of confidence by investors and the public in the strength of key financial institutions and markets ..." Banks are vulnerable to *loss of confidence* because they rely on short-term funding. This fear causes two problems. First, banks hoard their own cash and become especially reluctant to lend to other banks. Second, no financial institutions pull back their lending to banks to avoid any chance of being defaulted upon. These problems reinforce the fear and keep lending markets frozen. Elevated financing costs will slow growth. In the Great Depression, one-third of the U.S. banks failed, and the unemployment rate got to 25 per cent. The economy is going to be in for a rough period.

When speaking of the financial fallout on Wall Street, a local economics expert may have said it best." Economics is unfortunately not like chemistry or physics," said Randy Reynolds, senior vice president of First National Bank. "It's based on a million variables." As such, understanding the basics of Wall Street's financial crisis has been the goal of the year. Following is a general primer. The crux of the issue started with sub prime mortgages. Deregulation about five years ago allowed those with sub par credit, meaning someone who has a credit score of less than 620, to receive a loan. Moreover, banks and mortgage lending companies were no longer required to ascertain information like the applicant's income, nor were they asking applicants to put money down on their mortgages. But most sub prime loans came with a condition. Their interest rates were adjustable after a certain amount of time, unlike traditional loans whose interest rates are fixed for 30 years. After as little as six months, interest rates on sub prime mortgages changed – and many increased. But these home owners, many of whom should not have qualified for the loan, could not afford that increase. Either that or they couldn't afford the loan in the first place. Foreclosure was imminent.

Regardless of that risk, lenders were aggressive in approving these loans. Part of the impetus for them was the great demand for mortgage-backed securities in the global market.

A mortgage-backed security is a package of mortgages bundled together and then sold to an investor, like a bond. Foreign investors were hungry to invest in these securities because the U.S. housing market traditionally has been strong and stable.

It was so strong and stable that people were building houses en masse, with people buying second and third homes as investments. Moreover, housing prices were inflated greatly because of demand in strong markets, like Florida, California and Arizona.

Investment banking firms like Lehman Brothers and Bear Stearns bought these mortgage-backed securities – sometimes buying thousands of mortgages bundled together at a time. But now weak, sub prime mortgages were packaged together with stables ones.

Investment bankers didn't seem concerned. In order to buy the securities, they were borrowing money from another source, assuming a profit would be earned in selling them to an investor. As foreclosures piled up, investors were less eager to buy the mortgage-backed securities, and housing prices started to decline.

Because the investment banks were so tightly leveraged, as soon as the demand for the mortgage-backed securities fell, the companies were on the brink of bankruptcy, with all of their funds frozen: They didn't have money to lend and couldn't pay their loans (10).

Moody's Economy.com (Mark Zandi) estimates that all U.S. mortgage losses on existing mortgages will ultimately reach $650 billion. This $650b of mortgage default is miniscule in relation to the size of Government's vast financial resources and to the economy as a whole. It makes no economic sense that a $650 b problem would generate an $8 Trillion decrease in financial asset wealth over the last year (11).

ECONOMIC RECESSION

Recession is a condition in which the economic activities – production and consumption of goods and services decline. Economists disagree about the cause of recession. Some think that recession is set by decline in consumer spending, others point to decrease in capital investment, and still others blame government budget policy. But, in any event both capital investment and consumer spending decline during recession. Economic recession always starts in the capitalist countries where the bulk of the resources are concentrated in the hands of a handful of capitalists through systematic diversion of fund non-payment of bank loans by companies owned by the capitalists with strong support from the political authority and taking the money out of the banking system that makes the vast majority of the consumers fund starved thereby reducing the demand for goods and services and declining level of production and consumption. In such a situation, the governments of the capitalist domain never try to find the roots of economic recession and they try to divert the attention of the masses by one way or the other. Economic recession is the natural fall out of extreme level of exploitation which the capitalists perform in their everyday life with a varying degree. Recession does not come suddenly and it does not cause through exogenous forces. It occurs through the action of the powerful market forces from within the system. The roots of recession lie in the deregulatory, market oriented policies of liberal economic regime.

The immediate impact of recession is the piling up of goods waiting for buyers leading to falling of prices (deflation) with worsening joblessness for months and sometimes years together. The oil-rich countries of the Middle-East and the Persian Gulf which served for years as lifeline for many countries providing employment, sending dollars and tourists who filled up the hotels of western nations suddenly find themselves pulled into shrinking demand of their products and piling of huge oil stocks that led to dropping of oil prices and stock-markets across the globe causing panic among the investors. With reducing demand for their products, the people of the oil-rich nations defer going for tourism as also putting their money into stock-markets and initiate lying off workers creating an environment of joblessness and depression in most of the surrounding countries. The great economic depression that beset the United States and other countries in 1930's was unique in its magnitude and consequences with one American in every four was out job shaking the foundation of Western capitalism and the society based on it. The people with dwindling incomes were unable to pay their creditors taking the United States into economic breakdown. Most of the European countries were hit even harder. (12)

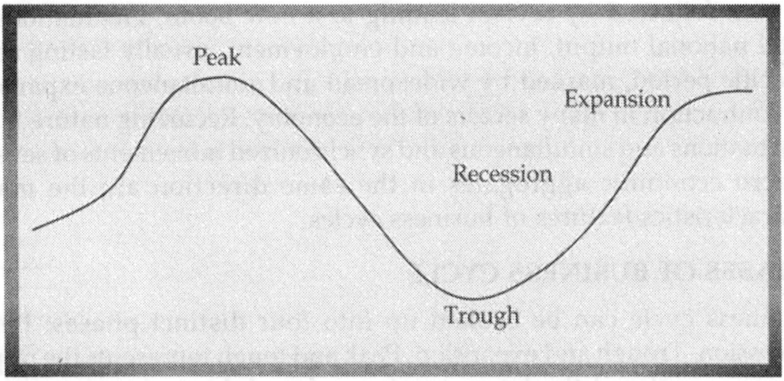

The fear of a recession looms over the United States. And as the clich goes, whenever the US sneezes, the world catches a cold. This is evident from the way the Indian markets crashed taking a cue from a probable recession in the US and a global economic slowdown. Weakening of the American economy is bad news, not just for India, but for the rest of the world too. A recession is a decline in a country's gross domestic product (GDP) growth for two or more consecutive quarters of a year. A recession is also preceded by several quarters of slowing down. An economy which grows over a period of time tends to slow down the growth as a part of the normal economic cycle. An economy typically expands for 6-10 years and tends to go into a recession for about six months to 2 years. A recession normally takes place when consumers lose confidence in the growth of the economy and spend less. This leads to a decreased demand for goods and services, which in turn leads to a decrease in production, lay-offs and a sharp rise in unemployment. Investors spend less as they fear stocks values will fall and thus stock markets fall on negative sentiment. (13)

They define a recession as the time when business activity has reached its peak and starts to fall until the time when business activity bottoms out. When the business activity starts to rise again it's called an expansionary period. To understand the above concept further, it is important to understand the concept of business cycles.

Business cycle refers to the periodic movements in the national income and output. The term cycle comes from the behaviour of these periodic movements. There is a period of rising output followed by a period of falling output, which is again followed by a rise in output. Many developed economies see such cyclical movements in their activity levels. Business conditions never remain steady. Prosperity and boom are generally followed by panic and depression, which are in turn followed by revival leading to a new boom. Fluctuations in total national output, income and employment, usually lasting for a specific period, marked by widespread and simultaneous expansion or contraction in many sectors of the economy. Recurring nature if the fluctuations and simultaneous and synchronized movements of several macro economic aggregates in the same direction are the major characteristics features of business cycles.

PHASES OF BUSINESS CYCLE

Business cycle can be broken up into four distinct phases: Peak, Recession, Trough and expansion. Peak and tough represents the upper turning point and the lower turning point of the cycle respectively. The peak is characterized by a high level of economic activity and is also referred to as the period of prosperity, while the trough is characterized by a very low level of economic activity and is also known as period of depression. Recession and expansion are the phases, which represents cumulative process, the former indicating a continuous movement on the downward direction while the expansion indicating a similar movement in the upward direction. During the phase of recession, production, employment, investment, profits prices are usually failing while in the phase of expansion all of them are usually rising. The phase of recession comes to an end at trough where the reversal of the cumulative process takes place and the phase of expansion begins. The expansion phase comes to end at the peak where again the reversal takes place and the phase of reversal begins. Thus each phase of the cycle passes into the next trough the operation of certain economic forces trough the operation of certain economic forces, which may be either internal or external to the basic system. (14)

Fresh economic data from the US has shown the recession in the world's largest economy is continuing to gather pace with house prices registering their biggest one month fall in 40 years. According to figures released on Tuesday, average house prices fell 14 per cent in November while sales of existing homes plunged by nearly nine per cent. Sale of new homes dropped by almost three per cent. Lawrence Yun, chief economist with the US National Association of Realtors, said the price drop was most likely the largest since the Great Depression of the 1930s.The grim news came on the same day that government figures showed US gross domestic product sliding by 0.5 per cent in the third quarter of the year. Data from the US commerce department also showed corporate profits falling 1.2 per cent during the quarter. The drop was the fifth straight quarterly decline and even worse than the 0.9 per cent decline estimated a month ago. At the same time data on US retail sales showed shoppers spending significantly less in the run-up to the Christmas holiday period than they did a year ago. The news brought more gloom to Wall Street, where the Dow Jones industrial average fell 1.18 per cent. That gloom spread to Asia on Wednesday with Tokyo's Nikkei share index down by 2.69 per cent in morning trade. Economists meanwhile are bracing for a steeper fall in US GDP of around six per cent in the current quarter, with further declines in the next six months before a lukewarm recovery takes hold, possibly in later 2009."It will get a lot worse before it gets better," said Nariman Behravesh, chief economist at Massachusetts-based forecasting firm IHS Global Insight. "We are in the midst of the worst recession in the post-war period, even factoring in a massive stimulus program. "With credit markets locked despite a $700 billion financial rescue package and billions of dollars in loans from the Federal Reserve, analysts see little likelihood of a quick turnaround in the housing market or the overall economy. Commenting on the latest GCP figures the Bush administration warned that the country should be prepared for worse news to come. "The fourth quarter, because of the credit crisis, the standstill in credit as markets froze up and the financial market turmoil will be significantly weaker," Tony Fratto, a presidential spokesman, told reporters at the White House. The plan is expected to include spending on infrastructure such as roads and bridges, aid to states, work to modernize schools and energy projects. (15)

It is completely incorrect to blatantly comment that all those economic happenings will take India to recession but night has a shade on it. Our Finance Minister's statement that "India has strong fundamentals" is very much correct and not all politically motivated. Our Central bank, The Reserve Bank of India also has expressed the same thing over and over again. Despite the rising Rupee adversely affecting their revenues, business projections announced by top outsourcing companies remain encouraging. Indian industry is currently seeing a cut in recruitment rate, reduced salary hikes, etc. this is surely going to be short-lived. Reduced exports due to US recession will actually make Indian producers & manufacturers turn to domestic market & serve its own people, and this will ultimately make the domestic market more lucrative for them. Performance of stock markets should not be regarded as some barometer for deciding the recessionary impacts, since stock markets players believe in philosophies of arbitrage and speculation and not purely economic happenings. But there is a need to closely watch and observe the situation and advance steps should be taken to reduce its effects in India as a growing economy with globalization. (16)

The United States of America (US or USA) is the world's largest economy. According to the CIA World Fact book, 2007 GDP is believed to be $13.84 trillion. This is three times the size of the next largest economy, Japan, which has a GDP of $4.4 trillion. US dominance has been eroded however by the creation of the European Union common market, which has an equivalent GDP of over $13 trillion, and by the rapid growth of the BRIC economies, in particular China, which is forecast to overtake the US in size within 30 years. The recent failure in the US housing and credit markets has resulted in a slowdown in the US economy. 2007 GDP growth was estimated at 2.2% but in 2008 it is projected to be just 0.9%, down from the 10-year average of 2.8% (see chart at end of article). In common with most developed countries, Services is the key sector of the economy. In 2007, services made up 78.5% of GDP, industry 20.5% and agriculture less than 1%. Around two-thirds of the total production of the country is driven by personal consumption. Although the US is often referred to as a free market economy, this is not entirely true, since there are government regulations protecting certain sectors, notably energy and agriculture. It can be more accurately described as a 'consumer economy'. Since the US economy is also the largest economy in the world, and the US consumer drives two thirds of the US economy, the US consumer is also a big driver of global economic activity. The forces of supply and demand directly drive the price levels of goods and services. What to produce, and how much of it is to be produced depends on the price level fixed by the interaction of supply and demand. The role of government in the US economy is crucial when it comes to decision-making regarding monetary and fiscal policies. The federal government takes all the necessary initiatives to ensure the growth and stability of the United States. The US government makes full use of economic tools such as money supply, tax rates, and credit control, among other things, to adjust the rate of economic growth. For the most part, the US Federal Government also regulates the operations of private business concerns in order to prevent monopolies. The government renders a number of direct services in the form of providing support for national defense, monetary aid for research and development programs, and funds for highway construction & infrastructure in general. The question of national debt is a controversial one within the US. At the start of 2008, the US federal debt stood at $9.2 trillion. This is a worrying 67% of GDP and equates to $79,000 for each American taxpayer, a number just over 117 million people. To add to the concern, American consumers are also increasingly dependent on debt and have been re-mortgaging their houses to higher loan amounts, and using the extra cash to fund high street purchases. This debt figure is the largest in the world in absolute terms, but as a percentage of GDP it is less than Japan and similar to several European countries. Most of the debt is funded by central banks and sovereign wealth funds from Asia, Europe and the Middle East. The largest and still the most important market in the world, the United States of America's economy is driven by consumers but is troubled by high debt levels. (17)

An economy which grows over a period of time tends to slow down the growth as a part of the normal economic cycle. An economy typically expands for 6-10 years and tends to go into a recession for about six months to 2 years. A recession normally takes place when consumers lose confidence in the growth of the economy and spend less.

This leads to a decreased demand for goods and services, which in turn leads to a decrease in production, lay-offs and a sharp rise in unemployment.

Investors spend less as they fear stocks values will fall and thus stock markets fall on negative sentiment. The economy and the stock market are closely related. The stock markets reflect the buoyancy of the economy. The Indian stock markets also crashed due to a slowdown in the US economy. (18)

The defaults on sub-prime mortgages (home loan defaults) have led to a major crisis in the US. Sub-prime is a high risk debt offered to people with poor credit worthiness or unstable incomes. Major Banks have landed in trouble after people could not pay back loans the housing market soared on the back of easy availability of loans. The realty sector boomed but could not sustain the momentum for long and it collapsed under the gargantuan weight of crippling loan defaults. Foreclosures spread like wildfire putting the US economy on shaky ground. This, coupled with rising oil prices at $100 a barrel, slowed down the growth of the economy. Tax cuts are the first step that a government fighting recessionary trends or a full-fledged recession proposes to do. In the current case, the then Bush government had proposed a $150-billion bailout package in tax cuts.

The government also hikes its spending to create more jobs and boost the manufacturing and services sectors and to prop up the economy. The government also takes steps to help the private sector come out of the crisis.(19)

Present financial crisis has its root in Friedman-Hayak prescription of unregulated market. Through this 'Market mantras,' the U.S. economies moved upward and experienced higher level of output, employment and income. Share prices went up. Investors used to reap handsome gain as dividends. It was all made possible by cutting edge designers of modern capitalism through hyper leveraging to the value assets. Debt equity ratio became very high. Debt financing was made the life-blood of economic activities. There was dramatic rise in share prices. Artificial rise in share prices without proportionate rise in real output has caused the house of card to tumble down.

HISTORY OF RECESSION

1. The US economy has suffered 10 recessions since the end of World War II. The Great Depression in the United was an economic slowdown, from 1930 to 1939. It was a decade of high unemployment, low profits, low prices of goods, and high poverty. The trade market was brought to a standstill, which consequently affected the world markets in the 1930s. Industries that suffered the most included agriculture, mining, and logging. In 1937, the American economy

unexpectedly fell, lasting through most of 1938. Production declined sharply, as did profits and employment. Unemployment jumped from 14.3 per cent in 1937 to 19.0 per cent in 1938. The people with dwindling incomes were unable to pay their creditors taking the United States into economic breakdown. Most of the European countries were hit even harder. The deepening of the great depression coincided with the end of the term of the then US President Herbert Hoover who opposed government intervention to control the mounting economic distress. Hoover's one major action, the creation of the Reconstruction Finance Corporation in 1932, to lend money to ailing companies was seen as inadequate that led to his defeat and election of Roosevelt as his successor. President Roosevelt, despite being a champion of free market economic regime, tried to bring increasing role of the government in economic activity and control of market and stimulate the economy through introduction of National Recovery Administration charged with establishing minimum wages and codes of fair competitions for stabilizing production and preventing price slashing that began in 1929. However, continued depression led to questioning the validity of his economic policies and political ideas leading to election of socialist writer Upton Sinclair as the Governor of California in 1934 with a programme for redistributing State's wealth. With world trade sliding downwards the countries turned towards nationalist economic policies and strengthened extreme right and left in politics helping Adolf Hitler to power in Germany and swelling left wing movements in other European countries creating massive insecurities among people and government contributing to tensions across the globe leading to 2nd World War. The massive military expenditure for the war that caused unprecedented death and destruction unfortunately provided the economic stimulus finally bringing the end of the depression. The great economic depression that beset the United States and other countries in 1930's was unique in its magnitude and consequences with one American in every four was out job shaking the foundation of Western capitalism and the society based on it. (20)

2. The US saw a recession during 1982-83 due to a tight monetary policy to control inflation and sharp correction to overproduction of the previous decade. This was followed by Black Monday in October 1987, when a stock market collapse saw the Dow Jones Industrial Average plunge by 22.6 per cent affecting the lives of millions of Americans.

3. The early 1990s saw a collapse of junk bonds and a financial crisis. The US saw one of its biggest recessions in 2001, ending ten years of growth, the longest expansion on record. From March to November 2001, employment dropped by almost 1.7 million. In the 1990-91 recessions, the GDP fell 1.5 per cent from its peak in the second quarter of 1990.

In 2001 and 2002, the Bush administration sought to boost the economy with a personal tax rebate that put between $300 and $600 in the hands of individual households and followed it up with tax incentives for businesses investing in plant and equipment. Treasury Secretary Henry Paulson made it clear that the administration believed that that policy not only worked, but worked quickly. This was seen as justifying the repeat performance. Between January 2001 and December 2002, the Dow Jones Industrial Average went down by 22.7 per cent, while the Sensex fell by 14.6 per cent. If the fall from the record highs reached is taken, the DJIA was down 30 per cent in December 2002 from the highs it hit in January 2000. In contrast, the Sensex was down 45 per cent. The whole of Asia would be hit by a recession as it depends on the US economy. Asia is yet to totally decouple itself (or be independent) from the rest of the world, say experts. The 2001 recession saw a 0.6 per cent decline from the peak in the fourth quarter of 2000. The dot-com burst hit the US economy and many developing countries as well. The economy also suffered after the 9/11 attacks. In 2001, investors' wealth dwindled as technology stock prices crashed.

The 2001 recession ran eight months. So did the 1990-91 contraction. The current economic slowdown, if it ends up being declared a recession, could challenge both of those to be longest since the 16-month recession in 1981-82. In dating the 2001 economic downturn, the *National Bureau of Economic Research* (NBER) committee's debate focused on how much emphasis to place on employment and GDP. It ultimately announced in November 2001 that the recession had started in March, when payrolls started declining. It made that call only after the government reported a GDP decline in the third quarter of 2001. (Later revisions showed that GDP declined during the first and third quarters of 2001.) But *the committee said at the time* that it "gives relatively little weight to real GDP because it is only measured quarterly and it is subject to continuing, large revisions." Payrolls continued declining into mid-2003, and the committee *declared the end of the 2001 recession in July 2003*. Using employment as a key gauge to declare the end of the recession could've meant a contraction running more than two years, the longest since the start of the Great Depression. In its *latest memo in October 2003*, the committee explained that it "views real GDP as the single best measure of aggregate economic activity" but also said it considers monthly figures to determine peaks and troughs.

A slowdown in the US economy is bad news for India. Indian companies have major outsourcing deals from the US. India's exports to the US have also grown substantially over the years. The India economy is likely to lose between 1 to 2 percentage points in GDP growth in the next fiscal year. Indian companies with big tickets deals in the US would see their profit margins shrinking.

The worries for exporters will grow as rupee strengthens further against the dollar. But experts note that the long-term prospects for India are stable. A weak dollar could bring more foreign money to Indian markets. Oil may get cheaper brining down inflation. A recession could bring down oil prices to $40. (21)

It would be worthwhile to see where the impact of the current recession stands *vis-a-vis* the previous ones and what the indications for the future are. Three major observations in this regard are:

First, the current recession is a confluence of all possible shocks; a housing bust coinciding with a severe credit crunch and a sharp equity bust, topped by inflationary shocks. Never before in the US history do we find such a queer confluence of all possible shocks.

Table 1
US Economy during Recessions

Recessions	*Great Depression*	*Oil Price Shock*	*Early 80s shock*	*Current crisis*
Tenure (/Months)	*Aug 29 - Mar 33*	*Nov 73 - Mar 75*	*Q180-Q380 & Q381-Q382*	*Dec. 2008 & So far*
Duration (months)	44	17	6 Quarters	11
GDP Loss (Peak-Trough)	-29	-310	-4.89	0.8
Cumulative GDP Loss	NA	-6.53	-11.05	NA
Manufacturing (ISM)	-45	-53.59	-21.91	-18.53
Consumption	–	-1.00	-0.54	-1.52
Residential Investment	–	-30.17	-35.46	-46.68
House price	–	-3.75	-4.77	-22
Equity price	-90	-29.51	-6.58	-52
Export	-30	3.86	-5.93	10.60
Import	-50	10.95	-11.10	4.54
Peak Unemployment	25	8.6	10.80	6.7

Source: Compiled from various US data including NBER

Second, its economic impact, particularly on leading indicators, is so far much sharper than what was typically observed in the past two severe recessions, but milder than what was observed during the Depression (Table). Housing prices have already corrected by about 22 per cent and the slide is continuing. The residential investment has halved from the peak of March 2006. The equity prices have corrected by over 50 per cent and are still falling. To top it all, credit crunch and contraction levels are unprecedented. This is only the beginning and it is yet to be known when and where the current trends bottom out.

Third, unemployment rate, which is a key recession indicator, has so far risen to 6.7 per cent, which is high in terms of absolute numbers.

Non-farm payrolls plummeted by 533,000 in November 2008, the worst decline since 1974, thereby taking the number of jobless to 1.9 million this year. The broad comparison conclusively establishes that the current recession is likely to be prolonged and painful than what was experienced during the 1970s and early 1980s. In other words, the recession can last longer than six quarters and the total economic and wealth loss might be huge. Our recovery chart, based on simulations, shows that the US may not return to the trend growth rate before 2011 or 2012 (Graph).

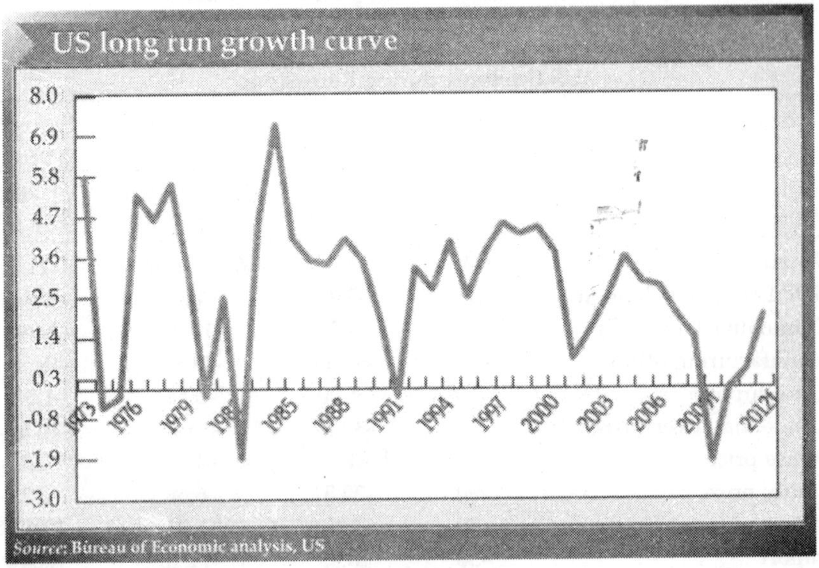

Graph 1

Source: *2008http://www.thehindubusinessline.com/2008/12/26/stories/2008122650410800.htm*

DIFFERENTIATING FACTORS

However, it is unlikely that it could be as bad as the Great Depression in terms of leading economic indicators. Unemployment rate is a key differentiator. While most predictions suggest that it may even reach 10 per cent this time, it is difficult to imagine unemployment rate touching 25 per cent as seen during the Great Depression. Another difference this time is the quick and active policy response from the Fed and the US government to contain the crisis. In contrast, these two kept feeding the crisis during first three years. It was only after Franklin Roosevelt's "New Deal' was put in place that the economy started recovering.

In fact, the recession was long due, as the up-cycle witnessed since 1991 was the longest one in the country's history. The US has excessively leveraged its economic and currency power during this period, not only to sustain its growth, but also to survive the 2001 crisis. But in the process it has created a double whammy of a $450-billion fiscal deficit and $850-billion trade deficit.

It is during this period, US households resorted to excessive spending and the banks to reckless lending. An average American's debt is now over 140 per cent of his disposable income. Similarly, some financial players have leveraged their assets to over 50 times. The de-leveraging process is in progress to correct this structural imbalance, but it may take a much longer time. This exercise itself is going to make the recession prolonged and painful. In a nutshell, the economic history shows that the US economy has already been over-harvested and, hence, needs a fairly long time to replenish. (22) Sudip Bandyopadhyay, director and CEO, Reliance Money has stated that "In the globalised world, complete decoupling is impossible. But India may remain relatively less affected by adverse global events." In fact, many small and medium companies have already started developing trade ties with China and European countries to ward off big losses. Manish Sonthalia, head, equity, Motilal Oswal Securities, says if the US economy contracts much more than anticipated, the whole world's GDP growth-which is estimated at 3.7 per cent by the IMF-will contract, and India would be no exception.

The only silver lining is that the recession will happen slowly, probably in six months or so. As of now, IT and IT-enabled services, textiles, jewelers, handicrafts and leather segments will suffer losses because of their trade link. Certain sections of commodities could face sharp impact due to the volatile nature of these sectors. C.J. George, managing director, Geojit Financial Services, says profits of lots of re-export firms may be affected. Countries like China import commodities from India do some value-addition and then export them to the US. The Indian IT industry will take a very big hit as their bottom line earnings will go down since major market in IT still remains the USA and there is a lot of dependence on the market .This would mean there would be the following impact; (23)

1. Employment rate will slow down and there could be a situation where fore cast hiring would virtually be stopped
2. The ITES sector will be hit under the belt as the low cost destination factor will no longer seem very attractive and there could be very drastic slow down in business in this sector
3. Call centers however will continue to thrive
4. The pay package in these industries will also take a hit with no increments and salary cuts.

The impact of a U.S. slowdown will be:

(a) A fall in commodity prices;

(b) Layoffs and the closure of factories will send the unemployment rate soaring, with the side effect of high benefits payments;

(c) With less money to spend, consumers will leave their wallets and credit cards at home, reducing retail sales. Sales of housing, cars and other big-ticket items will undergo a dramatic drop;

(d) Stock markets in upcoming months will perform miserably. The value of people's assets and other holdings will contract. They will be less likely to indulge in cruises or holidays or other extravagances;

(e) With less money all around, there will be less for the United States to spend on war on terror in Iraq and Afghanistan. It is possible that the United States may prematurely wind up and leave the war halfway;

(f) There may be a complete re-look at the North American Free Trade Agreement, which has moved jobs to Mexico and Canada;

(g) Unequal China trade, which has been a sore point for quite some time, may come under the scanner. The dollar-yuan currency relationship may be revised or, in the worst-case scenario, a few countervailing duties may be applied. In other words, a long-avoided protectionism may creep into the U.S. political thought process.

Apart from whatever happens in the United States, India and China will be at the receiving end of a few unpleasant jolts. China's ever-increasing exports to the United States may find an uneven reception. India may suffer the consequences of the withdrawal of investments from the stock market. The impact on India will be indirect. Globalization, in which India is a small fry, will impact it less. It is the institutional investors who will place India on the slippery slopes. In seven days including Jan. 21, the Indian stock market lost 8 per cent of its value. This translates to about US$400 billion of investors' paper money wiped out, or about two years of steady gains made by the little guys in the market.

One salient feature of India's spectacular economic performance in the last six years is that it is driven by domestic consumption. Not being dependent upon the United States makes the impact of the U.S. recession a bit more manageable. This is completely opposite for China, where exports drive the economy and domestic life may be ruined if orders dry up. India will have to worry about rapid interest rate cuts by the U.S. Federal Reserve Board. That would widen the gap between Indian and U.S. commercial interest rates, resulting in a capital outflow from U.S. to India where interest rates are still high. The arrival of excessive cash in India would not be welcome today. India would not know what to do with a huge inflow, and would have to cut its interest rates appropriately. Combine this with a weakening dollar and it would erode any export advantage. Hence additional rapid interest rate cuts by the Fed would require an appropriate response from India. (24)

What are the factors, which cause income, employment, investment, etc., fluctuate in a regular cyclical pattern? To explain these factors, a large number of theories have been put forward by various economists. A variety of factors such as fluctuations in money supply and bank credit, under consumption, overinvestment, clustering of innovations, interaction of the principles of the multiplier and accelerator, peoples expectation about the future etc., have been emphasized by different theories for explaining business cycles.

Various theories (factors) of business cycles can be broadly divided into two categories, external theories (factors) and internal theories (factors). In external factors, the basic cause of business cycles is found in events or factors outside the economic system like wars, revolutions, political events, growth and fluctuations in population, discoveries of new lands and resources, and finally scientific and technological innovations. The internal factors theorems emphasis on mechanisms or factors within the economic system such as money supply, over investment, under consumption, changes in consumption propensities and inducement to invest, etc., Many economists today agree that occurrence of business cycles is ideally explained, not by a single theory, but by a combination of theories, or more appropriately, but by a combination of external and internal theories.

One dominant practical explanation is linked to the expectations-linked behaviour of economic agents. Consider, for instance, a manufacturer. If he sees the level of activity going up, then he anticipates a higher demand for his goods in future and creates additional capacities. If all manufacturers think and act in a similar manner, the capacity addition is quite likely to overshoot what the demand can absorb. This leads to over-capacity, higher inventories, falling prices and consequently a decline in output. Similarly in a downward trend, the producers are likely to overreact and postpone their investments leading ultimately to an excess demand position. (25)

GLOBAL CONSEQUENCES

Financial convulsion which has appeared in America is threatening the economic stability of the whole world. To start with, after reaching the peak point of growth, there is a sudden slum in sales, shares, profit and property markets in U.S. liquidity preference. Consequently banks are worried, investors are disappointed. Surprisingly, over-optimism of Rergonomics has paved the way for pessimism. Crisis is seen by few as a beginning of the end of capitalism. Only time will tell the truth, it is failure of unregulated marked economy, none the less. Crisis is bringing in its wake a painful recession, which will cast its shadow over the whole world. Nobody claims to know what is going on? How far it will go or how to get out of it? M.W. Lee feels apprehensive about the result of recession and points out "A recession, once started, tends to build upon itself much as forest fire." It tends to create its own drafts and find internal impetus to its destructive ability." It goes on gathering momentum and finally gets transmitted to other parts of the world economy.

For U.S. and the world, this is not an unusual phenomena. IMF has listed 395 crises of different kinds relating to banks, debt and finance across the 161 countries of the world but at different scale and depth. However, there is unique feature that distinguishes the current unfolding crisis from the earlier crises. We live in an increasingly interdependent world, very much near to creating a unified global system. U.S.A. has acquired the status of global nerve centre of finance. Since, the crisis is spreading out from the U.S.A., it carries the germs of global consequences. Financial crises 'Made in America' brand is taken as global signal of financial troubles for other countries also. This has made the whole world extraordinary cautious. Leaders, economists, owner and management of the multinational companies are gearing themselves prudently to stop the rot from further expansion. (26)

According to the IMF, while all countries have been affected by the crisis the economies of advanced countries will shrink, while those of developing countries will continue to grow albeit at a much slower pace. The IMF estimates that in 2009 advanced countries will witness their sharpest ever contraction since the Second World War: The US. Economy will decline by 1.5 per cent, the Euro area countries by 2 per cent and Japan by 2.5 per cent. India, China and other developing counties, though continuing to be resilient, will suffer setbacks. The IMF expects China to grow by 6.75 per cent and India by just 5 per cent in 2009.

These features of the package notwithstanding, governments and investors outside the US hope that it would succeed in its prime intent—combating a US recession. This is because they rightly fear that if US does experience a sharp downturn, a global recession would follow. Some like the authors of the World Bank's annual Global Economic Prospects report for 2008 are more optimistic. They argue that global growth which slowed from 3.9 to 3.6 per cent between 2006 and 2007 would fall only marginally to 3.3 per cent in 2008. This is because "robust expansion in developing countries partly compensates for weaker results in high-income countries". Needless to say, the Bank itself senses an element of excessive optimism that derives from assuming that the processes of growth in developing and high-income economies are unrelated, leaving growth in the South insulated from any recession in the North, especially the US. It quickly goes on to say that: "Several serious downside risks cast a shadow over this soft landing for the global economy. External demand for the products of developing countries could weaken much more sharply and commodity prices could decline if the faltering US housing market or further financial turmoil were to push the United States into a recession. Alternatively, monetary authorities might overreact to the current climate of uncertainty and over stimulate the economy. This would be particularly dangerous for developing countries if the bulk of the resulting liquidity were to move into rapidly growing developing regions, provoking the same kind of overinvestment conditions that arose in the US housing market." (27)

Given the role of high growth in China and India in shoring up global growth, the impact of a US recession on the global economy would depend on the effects it would have on these two countries in particular. That could be significant given the dependence of growth in these countries on US demand. For over a decade now, China's merchandise exports to the US have amounted to a little more than a fifth of its merchandise exports to the world as a whole. And in India's case, while the share of merchandise exports to the US were at similar levels till 2002, they have been declining since and stood at 17 per cent in 2006. These are large proportions, and a recession in the US is bound to adversely affect the volume of exports and the pace of growth in these economies.

But even this does not capture the whole story. As Catherine Mann of the Institute for International Economics (27) puts it, "China is a value-added weigh-station for production ultimately destined for the United States and to a lesser extent Western Europe. To some degree the explosion in intraregional trade in Asia is not from 'home grown' demand, but rather still depends ultimately on exporting to the US market." That is, China is the location for the final reprocessing of capital goods, intermediates and raw materials imported into the country from elsewhere in Asia, before being sent on to the US. A slowing of exports to the US from China would slow the intra-regional trade in Asia that drives the region's growth. Further, in India's case, the US is also an extremely important market for its exports of services that have come to account for a large share of total exports from the country. In 2006-07, the exports of software and business services from India amounted to as much as 40 per cent of India's merchandise exports. Around two-thirds of these exports are directed to the Americas, especially the US. Here too, a slowdown in the US can have damaging consequences. The dependence on the US market of these two key developing country-drivers of global growth starkly illustrates the implications of a slowdown of growth in the US for the world economy. To believe therefore that a US recession would be partly compensated for by robust growth in these countries is to ignore the nature of global interdependence. Not surprisingly, most governments are willing to discount the implications of the America's efforts at combating recession for national and global inequality, so long as they serve to stall or reverse the downturn.

The World Bank's annual Global Economic Prospects report for 2008 is more optimistic. They argue that global growth, which slowed from 3.9 to 3.6 per cent between 2006 and 2007, would fall only marginally to 3.3 per cent in 2008. This is because "robust expansion in developing countries partly compensates for weaker results in high-income countries". (28)

1. US slowdown is always a bad news for the world, and India will also have to bear a part of that brunt. This is evident from the fact that Indian rupee has declined 6.2 per cent in the month of September against the Dollar and this is the biggest monthly drop since November 1997. Indian currency has risen more than 14 per cent against the US dollar in the past. An economy which grows over a period of time tends to slow down as a part of the normal economic cycle. The American recession was in waiting for quite sometime. The American GDP was already on decline for two or more consecutive quarters of a year. An economy typically expands for 6-10 years and tends to go into a recession for about six months to 2 years at the maximum if proper measures are in place to keep it from further escalating. The US economy accounts for 30 per cent of the world's GDP. The impact of an American recession on Indian IT industry - is quite on the cards. Indian companies have major outsourcing deals from the US. India's exports to the US have also grown substantially over the years; almost 75 per cent of its revenues come from the US. It is quite obvious that IT sector will be the worst hit. This development will force major IT companies to bring down their target on IT budgets. IT companies in India are already feeling the heat and have anticipated huge hole in their profit, some even losing their revenue with their client getting busted. To be candid US recession is likely to have an impact on the outsourcing industry, but it will happen slowly, maybe in six months or so. Under performing US companies like investment banks, law firms will affect the bottom line of the outsourcing industry. Small to medium size companies, which runs on a net margin of 7-8 per cent, will find it difficult to stay alive. How to keep the momentum going - Indian IT market will always have to feel the pinch if they are more US centric and fail to come out of this cocoon. The India IT management will need to focus and spend some time to develop markets in Middle-East-Asia and Europe or even local market. Business from this part of the world may offer possible short-term options to our export-dependent sectors. Diversification of trade in the Asian region or looking at domestic market will partly counter any drop in the US demand; In fact, many small and medium companies have already started developing trade ties with China and European countries to counter any loss.

2. Another best option for smart companies is to find markets in India itself to enhance productivity, though the deal sizes will be small and companies will have to re-negotiate their pricing. India has a huge, small and medium enterprise base and it is the right time to hit the bull's eye. It about those companies which are already addicted to American market and not willing to scale down will be in doldrums; even in that case we cannot blame them.
3. On the contrary some experts believe that India may remain relatively less affected by adverse global events." There is no threat to the skilled people. According to NASSCOM India will have a shortage of about 5 million skilled people in IT/ITeS. So there are lots of opportunities. To end on a positive note, it is believed that the Recession will not last long and it's just a part and parcel of growing economy.

It was as good as a red flag notice that the government is aware that India is not immune to the effects of the US slowdown and possible recession. "The US slowdown also has inflationary concerns," P. Chidamparam said, adding that further weakening of the dollar will portend problems for Indian exporters. The culprit, as always, is the one phrase that was the darling of economists around the world, globalization. That big inter-linkage of economic activity around the globe, which helped businesses source raw material, products, services and capital from anywhere, anyplace — the buzzword is now the bugbear.

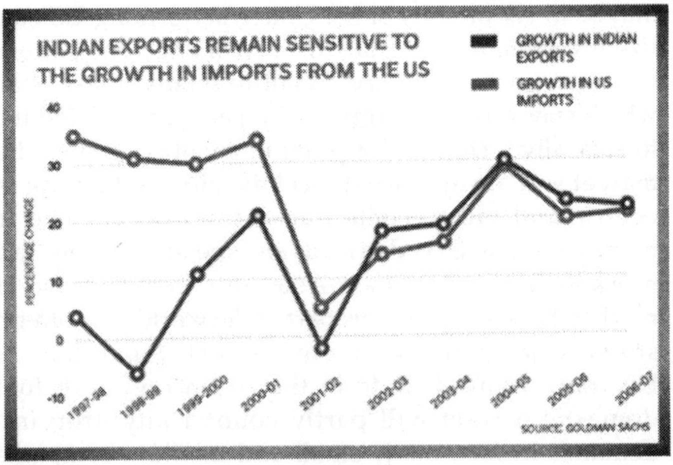

Graph 2

Source: http://www.tehelka.com/story_main37.asp?filename=Bu090208Will_Wall.asp

The links and, therefore, the impact, have been evident: on January 21, 2008, Martin Luther King day, US markets were closed — but there was a sell-off worldwide. India and Germany saw stock prices drop over 7 per cent, China and Britain had a 5 per cent fall and Japan a loss of 3 per cent. Export-oriented firms in other sectors are gearing up to face the crisis. South-India based Farida Shoes, which supplies footwear to Wal- Mart, JC Penny and Timberland, is trying to reduce dependence on the US market. "Initially, it will be housing, auto and white goods which will be affected. If the problem persists for another 12 months, then you will have problems in clothing and footwear," says Farida Shoes boss Rafique Ahmed. He has already cut his exposure to the US market from 50 per cent in late 2006 to 40-45 per cent: now, he'd like to slash it to around 30 per cent by the end of 2008, focusing more on Europe. Others are following suit, and trying to cut costs too. Ashok Kumar Jain, chairman, Carpet Export Promotion Council, says the industry is trying to innovate to offer cheaper products and retain cost competitiveness. "We are also organizing shows in newer markets of Latin America and European nations like Portugal and Turkey to increase our geographical reach," (29).

India's booming outsourcing industry may be hit due to the slowdown of the US economy, but not for long since the recession itself may not last more than two-three years, says Nobel laureate Amartya Sen. "A lot of our exports go actually to America, both commodity export but even more importantly our services they import. And these have slackened," Sen, who was in India to deliver a lecture in parliament, said in an interview. "There are some indications, clear indications, that the American growth-slack would hit India too. And, you know, our growth rate has come down a bit, and we have to see how much further it comes down," he said. "On the other hand, we are not thoroughly dependent on it. We should try to see what we can do to overcome that," Sen told senior journalist Kalyani Shankar in the interview to All India Radio. He said while there was nothing wrong in inter-country links in an increasingly globalizing world, India had to make sure that the ill-effects of slackening growth in America - or elsewhere - are reduced. (30)

The *World Bank's* just-published report, Global Economic Prospects 2008, predicts that the economies of developing countries like China and India "will play a crucial role in preventing the global economy from suffering a hard landing this year as the impact of the U.S. slowdown and turmoil in the credit markets continue...as those countries are taking over the baton of growth in the world economy. (31)

To a quarry on do you think the forthcoming US recession will have any impact on the Indian economy? Prime Minister Singh and [Finance Minister] P. Chidambaram are saying that the US recession won't have much of an impact, since India is not a substantial net exporter. It's true that we import more than we export. But if there's a recession in the United States it will push down prices for primary commodities. And if cash crop prices drop, that could lead to more farmer suicides. That's the trade effect: world prices for commodities go down relative to manufacturing prices, so peasants become impoverished unless there's a procurement scheme [price supports] or tariff protection. But the current government is following the WTO's neoliberal policy and gradually eliminating both tariff protections and procurement schemes. (32)

The world economic order is under threat by current crisis and before it is over, lot of blood will be shed in major centers or stock markets of the world. India will not be immune from this slowdown and will see many in cushy jobs being thrown out or shown yellow slips. The debate is not about its impact which is now an accepted fact, but about our ability to bear it and emerge out of it without major damage. There is a lot of talk about exports being not a major factor in our growth story nor foreign investment. For this we have to thank some who did not allow the present team to integrate Indian economy with free world or those who favoured free trade and free flow of capital into the country and its reverse as has been the case recently. We can talk about our banks remaining solvent because they were highly regulated. In other words all steps which looked like preventing our economy from growing are now helping us to fight the world-wide recession. Indian economy is not dependent on world markets for selling our products nor do we depend on them to feed our people. The subsidies which the supporters of free market wanted to be abolished are our strength today. It is time that we seriously look at policies like liberal imports of luxury goods which only make the poor feel worse off as display of riches in the midst of hungry people does not make for a stable economy nor a stable country. (33)

It quickly goes on to say that: "Several serious downside risks cast a shadow over this soft landing for the global economy. External demand for the products of developing countries could weaken much more sharply and commodity prices could decline if the faltering U.S. housing market or further financial turmoil were to push the United States into a recession. Alternatively, monetary authorities might overreact to the current climate of uncertainty and over stimulate the economy. This would be particularly dangerous for developing countries if the bulk of the resulting liquidity were to move into rapidly growing developing regions, provoking the same kind of overinvestment conditions that arose in the U.S. housing market." As Catherine Mann of the Institute for International Economics puts it, "China is a value-added weigh-station for production ultimately destined for the United States and to a lesser extent Western Europe. To some degree the explosion in intraregional trade in Asia is not from 'home grown' demand, but rather still depends ultimately on exporting to the U.S. market." That is, China is the location for the final reprocessing of capital goods, intermediates and raw materials imported into the country from elsewhere in Asia before being sent on to the U.S. A slowing of exports to the U.S. from China would slow the intra-regional trade in Asia that drives the region's growth. Further, in India's case, the U.S. is also an extremely important market for its services, which have come to account for a large share of total exports from the country. In 2006-07, software and business services amounted to as much as 40 per cent of India's merchandise exports. Around two-thirds of these exports are directed to the Americas, especially the U.S. Here, too, a slowdown in the U.S. can have damaging consequences. The dependence on the U.S. market of these two key developing country-drivers of global growth starkly illustrates the implications of a slowdown of growth in the U.S. for the world economy. To believe, therefore, that a U.S. recession would be partly compensated for by robust growth in these countries is to ignore the nature of global interdependence. Not surprisingly, most governments are willing to discount the implications of the Bush administration's efforts at combating recession for national and global inequality, so long as they serve to stall or reverse the downturn. (34)

India's booming outsourcing industry may be hit due to the slowdown of the US economy, but not for long since the recession itself may not last more than two-three years, says Nobel laureate Amartya Sen. "A lot of our exports go actually to America, both commodity export but even more importantly our services they import. And these have slackened," Sen, who was in India to deliver a lecture in parliament, said in an interview. "There are some indications, clear indications, that the American growth-slack would hit India too. And, you know, our growth rate has come down a bit, and we have to see how much further it comes down," he said. "On the other hand, we are not thoroughly dependent on it. We should try to see what we can do to overcome that," Sen told senior journalist Kalyani Shankar in the interview to All India Radio. He said while there was nothing wrong in inter-country links in an increasingly globalising world, India had to make sure that the ill-effects of slackening growth in America - or elsewhere - are reduced. (35)

The National Association of Software and Services Companies (NASSCOM) (36) hold a meeting in January 2008 to do a reality check amid rising global economic concerns: Is the Indian growth engine slowing down? Does India need to worry? How sharply will the US recession hit the nation? The meeting concluded partly on a note of optimism and partly on a note of caution. Consensus was found only on the matter that Indian companies and, indeed, the government will have to tackle the spectre of uncertainty in the coming days. For the first time in three years, India — Asia's third-largest economy — will grow at just over 7.1 per cent, although it will still remain the fastest growing nation after China among the world's biggest economies. High interest rates, lack of consumer demand for goods, skyrocketing real estate prices, rising rupee value, crashing stock market, declining exports in terms of value, soaring oil prices, and a looming US recession have all come together to create a situation which can cause a deceleration in the nation's galloping economy. India's gross domestic product is now forecast to grow at 8.7 per cent. Growth in the last financial year was at a stunning 9.6 per cent. Most economists believe that the US recession might still not hurt India too much as the country's economy is slightly decoupled from America's and also because India's domestic growth engine is powerful enough to churn up a high growth rate, with the spending power of its 300 million-strong middle class rising. India's growth can further accelerate if India's Finance Minister P Chidambaram takes necessary fiscal and monetary measures to boost higher growth, like beefing up government spending on social and infrastructure projects, cutting taxes to give more money to the masses to spend and getting the Reserve Bank of India to reduce interest rates. Economists at global investor DSP Merrill Lynch peg India's economic growth at just above 8 per cent, similar to that of rating agency Crisil, and merchant bankers JP Morgan, Yes Bank, and other financial institutions. None of them believe that India will face a recession similar to that of the United States. Yet, a slowdown is a slowdown and the nation needs to be ready with a plan to ride out the storm. In 2008, the stock markets reacted sharply to global economic concerns, with key emerging markets seeing their largest monthly fall in seven years, since September 2001. Almost every emerging market fell including Turkey (-24 per cent), China (-22 per cent), Russia (-16 per cent), India

(-14 per cent) and Korea (-14 per cent) after 2-3 years of sharp gains. "If the US were to go into a profound recession and the world does follow her in the deep pit, India may still grow 6.5 per cent," said Vijay Gaba, analyst with DSP Merrill Lynch in a latest research report to clients. But this is the worst-case scenario, which Merrill Lynch economists do not forecast. India's exports have already faced the brunt of a weak dollar, having decelerated 21.7 per cent during the April-December period last year from 23.9 per cent in the year to March 2007, hit by the strong rupee which rose 11 per cent against the dollar. India's software industry, which accounts for 5 per cent of gross domestic product and employs 2 million workers, also showed signs of strains. Shubhada Rao, chief economist with India's private sector new-age Yes Bank says, "We expect IT exports to slowdown between 10-15 per cent, simply based on expenditure cuts across the US as they deal with recessionary-type scenario. "India's latest industrial production data showed a growth of just 7.6 per cent in December last year, far below last year's double-digit expansion. The fall was due to a fall in manufacturing growth to 8.4 per cent from 14.5 per cent a year earlier. Yes Bank's Rao suggested that the move should be to boost infrastructure spending, which would bring momentum to goods, services, rural and urban housing sector.

CONCLUSION

The IMF's prescriptions, in its recent report January 28, 2009, are full of generalities. On measures to restore financial sector health, it urges stronger policy actions. Many countries have implemented several policy measures but a comprehensive framework for restoring financial health and dealing with bad assets remains to be built and the crisis has lingered. More aggressive and concerted actions are now needed through a unified approach involving liquidity provisions, capital injections and disposal of problems assets. On monetary policy, the IMF makes the point that as long financial conditions remain disrupted, the effectiveness of low interest rates to support activity will be limited. . It therefore urges central banks to rely increasingly on unconventional measures to unlock credit markets. Fiscal policy is constrained as deficits are widening sharply because of the cyclical downturn and the impact of asset price declines on revenues as well as stimulus measures and the cost of financial sector rescues. To prevent an adverse market reaction, the IMF urges policy makers to strengthen fiscal frameworks and commit to credible longer term policies that reverse the deficit buildup as economies recover.

Reference

Five Basic Needs of Human Beings, WEDNESDAY, OCTOBER 22, 2008HTTP://PAMYAU.BLOGSPOT.COM/2008/10/FIVE-BASIC-NEEDS-OF-HUMAN-BEINGS.HTML

Wikipedia

Robert E. Hall and Susan E. Woodward, 2008, ***http://sites.google.com/site/woodwardhall/***

Anitra L. Freeman (2008), ***http://anitraweb.org/homelessness/faqs/index.html,2008.***

Homelessness in the United, Wikipedia Free encyclopedia, States ***http://en.wikipedia.org/wiki/Homelessness_in_the_United_States#***

Luc Laeven and Fabian Valencia (2008), ***'Systemic banking crises: a new database'.*** International Monetary Fund Working Paper 08/224.

Paul Rye (2008), 'Ocean Insight/Shark poop causes 2008 financial crisis", Surfers village, Global Surf News, 8 October, ***http://www.surfersvillage.com/surfing/36822/news.htm***

Steven D. Levitt, 2008, Everything You Need to Know About the Financial Crisis: A Guest Post by Diamond and Kashyap, October 15, ***http://freakonomics.blogs.nytimes.com/***

Tara Kaprowy (2008), Root causes of financial crisis complicated, September 30, the Sentinel Echo, ***http://www.sentinel-echo.com/local/local_story_274154552.html***

PrintShare (2008) The U.S. Financial Crisis: A Misunderstanding of the Top Cause Delicious Digg Facebook reddit Technorati Steve Latter | Oct. 15, 2008 ***http://www.rgemonitor.com/us-monitor/254030/the_us_financial_crisis_a_misunderstanding_of_the_top_causes***

Global recession, its causes and impact ***http://newshopper.sulekha.com/newsitem/2008/12/global-recession-its-causes-and-impact.htm***

Mr. Tanveer Malik, Ms. Shweta Pandit, Impact of recession in American economy on India, ***http://www.fibre2fashion.com/industry-article/9/877/impact-of-recession-in-american-economy-on-india1.asp***

Prof. M. Guruprasad, Aicar Business School ***http://www.indiainfoline.com/Bschool/innernews.asp?storyId=71889&lmn=13***

US Recession Gathers Pace *UPDATED ON:WEDNESDAY, DECEMBER 24, 2008 06:13 MECCA TIME, 03:13 GMT* ***http://english.aljazeera.net/business/2008/12/200812240573440180 4.html***

The US Economy ***http://www.google.co.in*** *greenman, (2008) Will the US go into a recession?* on 16 Aug Vivid poster *Posts: 32 ,eToro member since:* 08 Aug 2008 *greenman, (2008) Will the US go into a recession?* on 16 Aug Vivid poster *Posts: 32 ,eToro member since*: 08 Aug 2008.

Arijit Bhattacharjee(2008), "Global recession, its causes and impact", December, , the Assame Tribune. *://www.thehindubusinessline.com/2008/12/26/stories/2008122650410800.htm*

US Recession: Prolonged and Painful? *Business Line, Business Daily* from *THE HINDU* group of ublications Friday, Dec 26, 2008 *http://www.thehindubusinessline.com/2008/12/26/stories/2008122650410800.htm http://www.ammas.com/topics/Economics/a147898.html*

Hari Sud (2008), "U.S. Recession will impact China and India, Column: Abroad View Published: February 05, *http://www.upiasia.com/Economics/2008/02/05/us_recession_will_impact_china_and_india/2058/*

Guruprasa, M, Aicar Business School *http://www.indiainfoline.com/Bschool/innernews.asp?storyId=71889&lmn=13*

Mahendra Singh (2009), "Global Financial Crisis: Its Impact"Opened on 4th January ,Gorkhapatra Sansthan - Dharmapath, Kathmandu, Nepal- *http://www.gorkhapatra.org.np/detail.php?article_id=12010&cat_id=7*

Chandrasekhar. C P (2008), "The Threat of Global Recession, People Democracy, Vol. XXXII, No. 05, February 04. *http://pd.cpim.org/2008/0204_pd/02042008_global.htm*

Jayan CM (2008), "How bad is US Slowdown-for IT India," - *http://www.bizsaga.com/item/2008/10/how-bad-is-us-slowdown-for-it-india*

Will Wall Street's Flu Make India Sneeze? *Tehelka Magazine, Vol 5, Issue 5, Dated Feb 9, 2008 http://www.tehelka.com/story_main37.asp?filename=Bu090208Will_Wall.asp* Sunday, 4 January 2009

Amartya Sen (2008), US Impact on Indian Outsourcing not for Long: 19 Aug, *http://timesofindia.indiatimes.com/Business/India_Business/US_impact_on_Indian_outsourcing_not_for_long_Amartya_Sen/articleshow/3379471.cms*

Edward M. Gomez (2008) *Guardian;* World Bank's report available *here.,* January 10 World Views a digest of International News and culture *http://www.sfgate.com/cgi-*

Prabhat Patnaik (2008), India: What Ails the Giant? - Interview with Jayati Vora, *http://www.pragoti.org/node/716,* Pragoti: Progress and Struggle.

Abhishek's (2008), *protect-poor-from-impact-of-recession/ WeblogOctober 28, ttp://waves.blog.co.in/2008/10/28/*

Chandrasekhar (2008), Recession threat "Column FrontlineVolume 25 - Issue 03 , Feb. 02-15, 2008, INDIA'S NATIONAL MAGAZINEfrom the publishers of THE HINDU *http://www.flonnet.com/fl2503/stories/20080215250305000.htm*

Amartya Sen Adverse US Impact on Indian Outsourcing not for Long: *http://www.hamaraphotos.com/news/politics/adverse-us-impact-on-indian-outsourcing-not-for-long-amartya-sen.html*

Indranil Mukherjee (2008), India Leadership Forum 2008, the annual summit of the National Association of Software and Services Companies, in Mumbai, Photograph: /AFP/Getty Images. First Published in India abroad, a Rediff publication. March 12, 2008 *http://specials.rediff.com/us/ia.htm.*

Joseph Stiglitz The Prominent Economist and the 2001 Nobel Prize winner, expressed that the U.S. may enter a recession due to the decline of house prices. Slowdown in US Housing Market and its Impact h*ttp://www.economywatch.com/economy-articles/us-housing-slowdown-impact.html*

Economics of Alternative Sources of Energy

LEELA BHASKAR*

Can you imagine life without lights, fans, cars, computers and Television, or of fetching water from the well and river? This is what life would have been like had not discovered the uses of energy - both renewable and nonrenewable sources.

Energy is a basic requirement for economic growth and social development and essential for all life - sustaining activities. While energy security has always been a key in concern in all countries, nations have become increasingly conscious of the challenge of ensuring the growth sector in an environmentally-benign manner.

Should India be looking at means to meet our energy requirements immediately or look for energy security in future to carry forward our development programmer? This question needs to be answered as the two requirements are different and will probably have to be answered differently. For instance if immediate energy needs are to be met by looking for sources for supply of crude oil and natural gas, in long run we will have to look for alternative sources of energy like non-conventional means of energy like wind power, sun energy an nuclear power The requirement for energy is no huge in case of India that we have to plan not for next few years but for several decades. No single source will be able to meet our needs so we must adopt a multi-pronged strategy. In the race for development and energy security most important factor will be flow of new technologies and it is no secret that most of the developments in this field will be made in the West. We, however, will have to use our talents and pool of scientists to adapt these technologies to suit our needs and requirements.

A country should choose an optimal mix between thermal, hydro, nuclear, renewable and non-conventional energy sources. In fact there

* Reader in Economics Ethiraj College for Women

is no standard prescription to choose this optimal mix, but it should be studied in detail specifically for each country as solution differs for every country. Thus, India has to choose its own mix and proceed accordingly. While economic considerations are one of the important inputs to choose such a mix, there are others too. For example, one of the reasons why Japan is going for Nuclear Power in a big way is to ensure energy security. This seems to be applicable for India also, especially in view of the technological control regime prevailing in the world.

The 'energy transformation' we are looking at will be different from any that the world has gone through in the past thousand years, in two profound ways. First, each of its predecessors-from animal to wind and water power in the tenth century, form wind and water to coal in the sixteenth to eighteenth, and from coal to oil in the nineteenth and twentieth—occurred spontaneously because the new energy source was so much cheaper and more versatile than the one it was replacing.

The second difference is that whereas earlier energy transformations went from one primary source to another, today there is no single prime energy source to which the world can shift from oil. For instance, nuclear energy can meet power needs but cannot become a raw material for the petrochemicals industry. In the foreseeable future at least, the world will therefore have to develop and rely upon a cocktail of energy sources. These could range from a return to coal, wind and water, to the development of new technologies to exploit biomass, solar and nuclear energy. Since natural endowments differ widely from country to country, each would do well to devise its own cocktail. The challenge before the developing countries is far more urgent because the speed with which they can reduce their dependence on oil will determine their future rate of growth. India was no exception then, but that is what has to change now and the sooner the better. The potential for harnessing alternate sources is immense.

The oil shocks of 1970s led to spiraling crude oil prices in the world market which prompted planners to view energy security as an issue of national strategic importance. Energy security has an important bearing on achieving national economic development goals and improving the quality of life of the people. India's dependence on crude oil will continue for most part of the 21st century but the continued dependence on crude oil is loaded against it with inherent price volatility linked to finite global reserves. In addition, global warming, caused largely by greenhouse gas emissions from fossil fuel energy generating systems, is also a major concern. India needs to develop alternate fuels considering the aforesaid two concerns.

The search for alternative fuels that would ensure sustainable development on the one hand and energy security on the other began in the 1970s itself. Consequently, new and renewable sources of energy have emerged as an option. The importance of increasing the use of renewable energy sources was recognized in India in the early 1970s. Ever since the 1980s emphasis has been laid on the development, trial and induction of renewable energy technologies for different sectors.

India has a policy framework in place to tap the potential for renewable energy such as solar, wind biomass, small hydro, irrespective of capacity. The Indian scientific establishment has been working on the development of various renewable energy technologies/systems. In 1981, the Government established a Commission for Additional Sources of Energy (CASE) in the Department of Science and Technology, on the lines of the Space and Atomic Energy Commissions. The mandate of CASE is to promote R&D activities in this area. In 1982, CASE was incorporated in the newly created Department of Non-Conventional Energy Sources (DNES), which in 1992 became the Ministry of Non-Conventional Energy Sources (MNES). India is the only country in the world that has an exclusive Ministry which deals with new and renewable energy sources.

MNES supports the implementation of a large broad-spectrum of programmes covering the entire range of new and renewable energies. The programme broadly seeks to, Inter-alia, supplement conventional fossil fuel-based power, and reach renewable energy, including electricity to remote rural areas for a variety of applications like water pumping for irrigation and drinking water purposes, drying farm produce, improved chulhas and biogas plants, energy recovery from the urban, municipal and industrial wastes. In addition, exploitation of hydrogen energy, geothermal energy, tidal energy and biofuels for power generation and automotive applications is also envisaged.

The Electricity Act 2003 contains several provisions to promote the accelerated development of power generation from non-conventional sources. The Electricity Act 2003 provides that co-generation and generation of electricity for renewable sources would be promoted by the SERCs by providing suitable measures for connectivity with grid and sale of electricity to any person and also by specifying, for purchase of electricity for such sources, a per cent age of the total consumption of electricity in the e area of distribution licensee.

As a rapidly developing country, India's energy needs are likely to balloon over the coming decades. How and in what areas these needs materalise will depend on five major factors.

First, these energy needs will be driven by India's quest to maintain the high level of economic growth (around 6 to 7 per cent annually) that it has enjoyed since 1994.

Second, much will depend on India's ability (or lack thereof) to locate and use existing domestic gas and petroleum reserves.

The third will be the ability of the Indian political system to address certain structural inefficiencies which contribute to significant loss and wastage.

Fourth, it will also depend on its ability to adopt new and more energy efficient technologies.

And fifth, much depends on India's ability to secure external sources of energy.

Conventional energy sources based on oil, coal, and natural gas have proven to be highly effective drivers of economic progress, but at the same time damaging to the environment and to Human health. The potential of renewable energy sources is enormous as they can in principle meet many times the world's energy demand. Renewable energy sources such as biomass, wind, solar, hydropower, and geothermal can provides sustainable energy services, based on the use of routinely available, indigenous resources.

A transition to renewable-based energy systems is looking increasingly likely as the costs of solar and wind power systems have dropped substantially in the past 30 years, and continue to decline, while the price of oil and gas continue to fluctuate. In fact, fossil fuel and renewable energy prices, social and environmental costs are heading in opposite directions. Furthermore, the economic and policy mechanisms needed to support the widespread dissemination and sustainable markets for renewable energy systems have also rapidly evolved. It is becoming clear that future growth in the energy sector is primarily in the new regime of renewable, and to some extent natural gas-based in conventional oil and coal sources. Financial markets are awakening to the future growth potential of renewable and other new energy technologies, and other new energy technologies, and this is a likely harbinger of the economic reality of truly competitive renewable energy systems.

Biomass is the term used for all organic material originating form plants (including algae), trees and crops and is essentially the collection and storage of the sun's energy through photosynthesis. Biomass energy or bio energy is the conversion of biomass into useful forms of energy such as heat electricity and liquid fuels. Modernized biomass energy is projected to play a major role in the future global energy supply. This is being driven not so much by the depletion of fossil fuels, which has ceased to be a defining issue with the discovery of new oil and gas reserves and the large existing coal resources, but rather by the recognized threat of global climate change, caused largely by the burning of fossil fuels. Its carbon neutrality (when produced sustain ably) and its relatively even geographical distribution coupled with the expected growth in energy demand in developing countries, where affordable alternatives are not often available, make it a promising energy source in many regions of the world for the 21st century.

In general renewable forms of energy are considered "green" because they cause little depletion of the Earth's resources, have beneficial environmental impacts, and cause negligible emissions during power generation. Yet, while biomass is in principle renewable and can have positive environmental impacts if managed properly it also shares many a characteristics with fossil fuels, both good and bad. While it can be transported and stored allowing for heat and power generation on demand, modernized bio energy can also have negative environmental impacts associated both with the growing of the biomass and with its conversion to energy carries.

Wind has considerable potential as a global clean energy source, being both widely available, though diffuse and producing no pollution during power generation. Wind energy has been one of humanity's primary energy sources for transporting goods, milling grain, and pumping water for several millennia. From windmills used in China, India and Persia over 2000 years age to the generation of electricity in the early 20th century in Europe and North America wind energy has played an important part in our recorded history. As industrialization took place in Europe then in America, wind power generation declined, first gradually as the use petroleum and coal, both cheaper and more reliable energy sources, became widespread and then more sharply as power transmission lines were extended into most rural areas of industrialized countries. The oil crises of the 70's, however, triggered renewed interest in wind energy technology for grid connected electricity production, water pumping and power supply in remote areas, promoting the industry's rebirth.

Among the developing countries India continues to be the leader followed by China. India was one of the fastest growing wind markets in the mid-90s but has since slowed substantially due to under performance of projects (often due to poor siting), transmission problems, and political and economic instability, all of which have affected investments in new projects. Extensive use of investment tax credits has also liked to unsustainable revenue losses for the government. During the 1990s electricity consumption more than doubled in India, and despite huge expenditure in the power industry, the country still has 12 per cent electricity deficit and 20 per cent peak power shortage. Due to these conditions, and the continued fast rate of growth in consumption, India continues to be considered a key market for wind developers China remains mostly an untapped market with a huge future potential for wind energy. They have invested relatively little money into projects to date, which remain small and donor based. It is expected that major commercial development, possibly to take place in the next decade, will be needed for strong wind energy development to occur in China.

There are two basic a categories of technologies that convert sunlight into useful forms of energy, aside from biomass-based systems that do this in a broader sense by using photosynthesis from plants an intermediate step. First, solar photovoltaic (PV) modules convert sunlight directly into electricity. Second solar thermal power systems use focused solar radiation to produce steam, which is then used to turn a turbine producing electricity. The following provides a brief overview of these technologies, along with their current commercial status.

Hydropower is a significant, source of electricity world wide and will likely continue to grow especially in the developing countries. While large dams have become much riskier investment there still remains much unexploited potential for small hydro projects around the world. It is expected that growth of hydroelectricity will continue but at a slower rate than that of the 70's and 80's. Thus, the fraction of hydroelectricity in the portfolio of primary sources of energy, which is today at 19 per cent, is expected to decrease in the future. Improvements and efficiency measures are needed in dam structures, turbines, generators, substations, transmission line, and environmental mitigation technology if hydropower's role as a clean renewable energy source is to continue to be supported.

We conclude that current energy producers are in the best position to capture new renewable energy markets. These producers have the capital needed to make forays into these markets, and the most to lose if they do not invest and renewable energy technologies continue to flourish. We believe that artful introduction and integration of renewable energy technologies into energy production systems, along with encouragement form the public sector where appropriate can provide a path that eventually leads to heavy reliance on renewable energy systems into the future. This future would be more environmentally and socially sustainable than one we would achieve by following a more "conservative" path based on continued reliance on fossil fuels. This latter path in many ways implies higher risks to human and ecological health and welfare over time, and it is a path that is increasingly difficult to justify based on the performance that renewable are now achieving.

The increase in greenhouse gas emissions and the resulting climatic changes, which occur globally, have understandably caused world-wide concern. According to a assessment by the intergovernmental panel on Climate Change, the rise in the average temperature by the end of the next century i.e., 2100 will be between 1 degree to 3.5 degrees C. This has serous implications for the entire ecosystem of the world. This fact has led to a series of initiatives at international levels to develop eco-friendly alternatives that would meet the needs of the present generation without compromising the abilities of the future generations.

The developed nations have contributed a greater share of the emissions of carbon dioxide, leading to global warning. But the current trends in the developing nations are very alarming and, if unchecked, developing countries will contribute half of the annual greenhouse gases. This calls for urgent measures for minimizing, if not replacing, the reliance on fossil fuels to meet the increasing energy 7 requirements. It is for this reason that the non-conventional renewable sources of energy have caught the attention of many.

There has been a growing awareness of the benefits of renewable energy, mainly on account of sustained public awareness generation campaigns. Outlays have been provided in the 10th Plan to achieve the aim of electrification of around 25,000 remote unelectrified villages and hamlets by 2007. In addition, it is expected that the share of renewable power in the power generation capacity to be added during the 10th and 11th plan periods would be around 10%.

Efforts are being made to reduce the capital cost of projects based on non-conventional and renewable sources of energy, reduce cost of energy by promoting competition with in such projects and at the same time, taking adequate promotional measures for development of technologies and a sustained growth of these sources. The efforts to increase the share of renewable in the total power generation capacity of the country have yielded results. The share has been continually rising. Renewable presently contribute about 4800 MW, which represents over 4.5% of the total installed capacity. The power generation capacity established so far has largely come about through private investments. Wind power contribute about 2483 MW, while biomass power and cogeneration account for 613 MW and the share of small hydropower is 1603 MW. With the present fossil fuel (coal, oil and natural gas) potential unable to meet the current demands, renewable resources of energy provide viable alternatives. With a cycling time of less than 100 years, renewable resources, if optimally utilized, can fill the void created by the depleting non-renewable resources which take more than a million years to get replenished.

The current sources of renewable are form wind, small hydro, solar biomass, energy from wastes (such as biogas, agro wastes, etc). However, not many people know that traditional fuels account for 53.2 per cent of total energy consumption in Karnataka.

Many villages have been supplies with efficient fuel stoves and bio gas digesters by the government but lack of maintenance and unawareness on the part of the villagers has led to the skewed presumption that the technology has failed", said Mr. T. V. Ram Chandra. Other than using residues from forests, agriculture, horticulture and livestock, scientists also propose energy plantations. In other words, growing select species of trees and shrubs that are harvestable in a comparatively shorter time and can be used as efficient fuels. "The heat content of the wood is similar to the wood is similar t that of Indian coal", Scientists say.

A British statesman had once remarked, "The Kingdom of heaven runs on righteousness, but the kingdom of earth runs on oil". It's still true today and despite the hopes for alternative energy sources nothing has challenged the dominance of black gold. In fact of the growing threat of global warming. India needs to take urgent steps to an alternative energy sources. Above all we need to create an alternative energy system within a few years to take over form oil so that what is left will last longer and be put to more valuable uses.

Already India is the world's sixth-largest consumer of energy. Most estimates suggest that to sustain its current average annual growth rate it will need to increase its energy consumption by about 4 per cent annually.

Currently, domestically mined coal meets close to 70 per cent of India's energy needs; after China and the United States, India is the world's third-largest producer of hard coal. Oil supplies about another 30 per cent of the country's energy.

Currently, India imports more than 60 per cent of its annual oil needs, or slightly more than 1.4 million barrels of oil per day. At current rates of economic growth this figure is likely to rise to as much as 5 million barrels per day by the year 2020.

Unless India obtains or develops alternative sources of energy, in 15 years it will have to import close to 90 per cent of its petroleum needs.

Our dependence on fossil fuels might continue for most part of the 21st century. But our oil reserves may not last longer than 2025 and coal reserves which were earlier expected to last for another 200 years May now not last long. Energy security has an important bearing on the achievement of national economic development goals and raising quality of life. The level of per capita energy consumption has for long been considered as one of the key indicators of development. Development on crude oil in a situation where its price is volatile and availability finite has to be shaken cff. India needs to develop alternate fuels to counter the problem.

Noting that the return from huge investments in developing energy sources was "far from adequate", *Prime Minister Man Mohan Singh* on Jan. 03, 2007, Wednesday asked scientists and engineers to find alternative sources of energy supply and energy conservation technologies.

> "The purpose of this whole initiative, and beginning with countries like India, is to recognize that alternative sources of energy are going to be important for the development of clean world and a world that becomes substantially les reliant on non-renewable sources of energy", Bush said.
>
> India on the lookout for alternative energy sources.

According to recent report by Wall Street Journal, energy hungry India is seeking alternative fuels to complement its booming demand.

In additional expanding local oil and gas production India has been encouraging use of renewable, more environment-friendly fuels like hydro, solar and wind power to cut reliance on thermal power that makes two-thirds of India's electricity.

More importantly, it aims to boost nuclear-power output nearly tenfold by 2020, even though a new nuclear-power plant costs five times more than a coal or oil-fired one.

In July of this year, the United States said it would share its civil nuclear technology with India. And just this week, India and France agreed to negotiate a pact to cooperate on nuclear power.

Expansion of the hydropower sector, which meets around 20% of power needs now, will be more modest. The government aims to lift current hydropower capacity of 23,488 megawatts by 50,000 megawatts by 2017.

On purchasing Power Parity (PPP) basis, we in India have one of the highest energy prices. In 2002 Indian industries paid 45 per cent KWH, as opposed to 20 cents in China and 2 per cent in the US on PPP basis this is affecting our competitiveness. It will force us to reduce other costs, affecting the compensation paid to workers. Integrated Energy Policy Report (IPER) has attempted to ensure adequate supply of energy at the least possible cost by meeting another challenge of providing clean and convenient 'lifeline energy to the poor. This can happen only if the recommendations of the report are implemented. Other wise our current energy crisis will only worsen. While arriving at the demand, IPER has estimated that to achieve GNP growth supplies 8 to 10 per cent, commercial energy supplies have to increase at the rate of 5.2 per cent this is a heroic assumption. Based on the actual performance of the economy between 1980 and 2003, this energy elasticity's would have been between 8.6 per cent and 10.8 per cent. This implies that the Indian economy will succeed in adopting state of the art energy technologies and hitherto unsuccessful conservation measures.

India's dependency on non-commercial energy is as high as 35 per cent reducing it to less than 10 per cent by 2031 will not be easy. We need extra ordinary efforts to achieve the low energy elastic ties that are forecast.

References

American Wind Energy Association (200), "Wind Energy Fact Sheet: Comparative costs of Wind and other Fuels "and "Global Wind Energy Market Report": *URL: http://www.awea.org*. [The American Wind Energy Association(AWEA) is a national trade association, representing wind power Poland developers, wind turbine manufactures, utilities, consultants, insurers, financiers, researchers and others involved in the wind industry, that promotes wind energy as a clears source of electricity for consumers around the word].

Duke, R. D. and Kammen D. M. (1999), "The Economics of Energy Market Transformation Initiatives", *The Energy Journal*, 20(4), 15-64 [An Economic analysis of market transformation programs for the energy sector, showing that such programs can potentially have attractive benefit to cost ratios once the effects of reducing technology casts are considered.]

Hall D.O. and Scrase, J. I. (1998), "Will Biomass be the environmentally friendly fuel of the future?" Biomass and Bioenergy, 15 (4/4); 357-367. [Article analyzing the future using life-cycle analysis and evaluation of external costs.

Shell Petroleum (2000), 'Global Scenarios: 1993-2020", Summary Brochure. [Shell petroleum's scenario forecast of major fuel sources for electricity production for the OECD through.

U.S. Department of Energy (1997), Renewable Energy Technology Characterizations, Topical Report prepared by U.S DOE Office of utility Technologies and EPRI, Tr- 109496. Dec. [A comprehensive assessment of renewable energy technologies, including technical descriptions, potential applications, and cost assessments and forecasts].

Sumit Ganguly; India need energy and the U.S. SEP. 2, 2005.................NEWS

Ashish Mehta (2003),Answer to Energy Shortage in India would be Wind, December 20.

Laxmi Devi, *Economic Times,* June 29 2005

Prem Shnakar Jha; Alternative Sources Needed. Deccan Herald, Feb. 17, 2005.

Bhamy V. Shenoy (2007), Sep. 15, Industrial Economist.

Economics of Health Insurance in India#

J. SRINIVASAN*

INTRODUCTION

From an economic perspective insurance is a financial intermediation function by which individuals are exposed to a specified contingency. Each contributes to a pool from which participating individuals are paid. On the other hand, from a legal perspective insurance is an agreement, the insurance policy or insurance contract, by which one party, the policy owner, pays a stipulated consideration called the premium to the other party, called the insurer, in return for which the insurer agrees to pay a defined amount or money or provide a defined service; when referring to life insurance it is often understood to include all four classes of insurance coverages namely,

(a) death – usually called life insurance or life assurance

(b) Living a certain length of time – called endowments, annuities and pensions

(c) incapacity – called disability and long-term care insurance

(d) injury or incurring a disease – called health insurance, accident insurance and medical expense insurance.

Medical expenses normally fall into the fourth category – policies covering the costs of injuries or sickness – and sometimes, also in the third category or coverages – policies that pay benefits because of physical or mental incapacity.

Paper Presented in the 89th IEA Annual Conference, Kurukshetra University, December 20-22, 2006.

* Reader in Economics at Pondicherry University, Pondicherry-605 014.

However, in this paper, the term health insurance to mean any form of insurance whose payment is contingent on the insured incurring additional expenses or losing income because of incapacity or loss or good health.

CATEGORIES OF LIFE AND HEALTH INSURANCE

Much life and health insurance is purchased as group insurance, typically by employers for the benefit of their employees. Industrial insurance includes life and health insurance policies issued to individuals in small amounts. Ordinary insurance includes individual life and health insurance policies whose benefit amounts are larger than industrial insurance. Premium are payable monthly or less frequently. Finally, some life and health insurance - referred to as credit insurance - is issued through lending institutions to cover debtors' obligations if, they die or become disabled.

All important operations, practices and regulation relate to economics. Conditions for a perfectly competitive insurance market are (1) A sufficiently large number of buyers and sellers such that no one buyer or seller nor any group of them can influence the market. (2) Sellers have freedom of entry into and exit from the market (3) Sellers produce identical products and (4) Buyers and Sellers are well informed about the products.

In this paper, an attempt has been made to present a theoretical frame work to analyse the economic problems that are related to life and Health Insurance. This paper covers the categories of Insurance market imperfection, the economic basis for life ant health insurance- The demand for life and Health Insurance, The Human Life Value Concept, Huebner's Qualitative and Quantitative dimensions of the Human Life value, The Production of Life and Health Insurance and Insurance Production Process.

The plan of this paper is as follows: Section 2 provides the theoretical framework, covering the economic basis for life and Health Insurance; The demand for Life and Health Insurance; Section 3 introduces the concept of Human Life Value (HLV) along with its qualitative and quantitative facets of the Human Life Value; and the production of Life and Health Insurance and Insurance Production Process. Section 4 discusses the status of health insurance in India. Finally, conclusion of the paper is given in section 5.

SECTION-2

ECONOMIC BASIS FOR LIFE AND HEALTH INSURANCE

Market Power

Market Power in insurance markets relates most exclusively to Sellers and can arise in atleast four ways:

- Barriers to entry or exit
- Economies of Scale or Scope
- Price Discrimination
- Product differentiation

If a market has barriers to entry or exit, suppliers have market power. For example, we would not ignore a group of health insurance companies that agreed to set prices or apportion a geographic area among themselves. Economics of scale exists when a firm's average cost of production falls with increasing production. Economies of scale constitute another kind of entry barrier. The Minimum Efficient Scale (MES) refers to a certain firm size where further growth yields no additional efficiency. Economies of scope exist when a single firm can produce multiple products or services at lower costs, than in multiple firms.

Price Discrimination occurs when a firm offers effectively identical products at different prices to different groups of customers. Hence, the firm can gain market power, which implies that higher profits. Product differentiation prevails when buyer prefer one firm's products over those of its rivals. This may be due perceived differences in product quality, service reputation, convenience or other attributes.

Both negative and positive externalities exist in life and health insurance. Externalities can occur when a firm's production or an individual's consumption has direct and uncompensated effect on others. If others benefit, we have a positive externality. If costs are imposed on other, we have a negative externality.

Some collectively consumed goods and services that are desired by the public - called public goods - carry extensive positive externalities. When such goods and services are available to others at low or zero cost, they can cause a free rider problem. To cite a few examples - public education, lighthouses, police and fire protection etc.

Information Problems: Asymmetric information problem arise when one party to a transaction has relevant information that other does not have. From classes of such problems exist:

- "Lemons" Problems
- adverse selection problems
- moral hazard problems
- principal - agent problems

Economists refer "lemons" problem to a situation in which the insurance customer knows than the seller about the seller and its products. Adverse selection problems – in which the customer knows more than the seller about the customer's situation.

The Demand for Life and Health Insurance

The Concept of Human Capital

Economists since Adam Smith have recognized that people are important elements of nations' wealth. The essence of human capital is that investments are made in oneself with an expectation of future benefits. Economic research related to investment in human capital has recently gained substantial recognition. Indeed, the 1991 Nobel Memorial Prize for economics was awarded to Gary S. Becker for his pioneering research on human capital. Investment in human capital-education, for example-has become one of the most cogent explanations for the differences in countries' rates of economic growth as well as differences in wage rates between and within countries[1].

Estimating the value of human capital is complicated by the necessity to distinguish between expenditures for consumption and investment. Much of what is called consumption constitutes investment in human capital. Thus, expenditures on education, health, and migration to take advantage of better job opportunities are examples, as are workers acquiring on-the-job training. In these and other ways, the quality of human effort is greatly improved and productivity is enhanced.

One method for estimating human capital depends on its yield rather than its cost. The marketplace tends to reflect investment in personal development through wages and salaries. The resulting increase in earnings is viewed as the yield on the investment. Thus, those with university degrees typically earn more than those without them. This earnings differential can be thought of as the return on an investment in education.

Economic Theories of Consumption

Each consumption theory begins with the assumption that rational consumers seek to maximize their lifetime utility. Utility is a measure of consumer satisfaction derived from economic goods. Individuals seek to maximize their utility and minimize their disutility over their affairs to derive maximum enjoyment (and minimum discomfort) throughout their lives.

The maximization of lifetime utility, therefore, involves attempts by consumers to allocate their lifetime incomes in such a way as to achieve an optimum lifetime pattern of consumption. This means planning for the future and not living only for today. This concept is rational but on what basis would we expect individuals to make allocations between now and the future or, stated differently, between consumption now and consumption (saving) for the future? The economic literature has four hypotheses, these are the following:

- the absolute income hypothesis
- the relative income hypothesis
- the life cycle hypothesis
- the permanent income hypothesis.

Consumption Theories and Insurance

In their earliest forms, none of the consumption theories appropriately allowed for the possibility of bequests to heirs or for an uncertain time of death. Obviously, these two extensions make the theories more relevant.

In this seminal paper, Yaari examined the role of insurance within the context of the life cycle model by including the risk of dying. He showed conceptually that an individual increases expected lifetime utility by purchasing fair life insurance and fair annuities.[2] "Fair" means paying a premium equal to the expected value of payments to or on behalf of the individual, without charges for expenses or profits.

Pissarides extended Yarri's work by examining the joint motivation of saving for retirement and for bequests via life insurance.[3] He proved that life insurance was theoretically capable of absorbing all fluctuations in lifetime income and, thereby, could enable consumption and bequests to be independent of the timing of income. As a result, the same effective consumption pattern could be achieved through the appropriate use of life insurance as could be achieved if the time of death were known with certainly. Without life insurance, the lifetime consumption pattern would be different and involve less enjoyment (utility).

Lewis included the preferences of those dependent on the breadwinner's income. His empirical estimates based on U.S. households were encouraging. He found that life insurance ownership was positively related to household income and to the number of dependent children. An important conclusion of his research was that social security substituted for privately purchased life insurance.

The Production of Life and Health Insurance

Our intention here is to provide an overview of how the insurance supply evolves. Insurance supply is a function of price, the higher the unit price, the greater will be the quantity supplied. However, the supply of insurance is not subject to direct assessment because insurance output is not subject to precise definition or measurement. Even so, we know that insurance supply-however defined-is positively related to insurer risk-bearing capacity. Risk-bearing capacity, in turn, depends on insurance capital, that is the difference between assets and liabilities. Of course, insurer technique expertise and management capabilities also are important factors in determining insurance supply.

The production of insurance services-as with other financial services-relies on financial and human capital. Financial capital underpins all operations. The most important operations in the production process include insurance pricing, underwriting, and claims handling; investment management: and distribution.

Insurance Production Process

The principal technical elements of the insurance production process (manufacturing) related to pricing, underwriting, and claims handling. Actuaries determine insurance premiums and necessary reserves using their best estimates of future losses and expenses, with an eye toward competitiveness.

Because of time lags between the receipt of premiums and loss payments, the competitive premium will be the present value of expected losses, expenses, and profits. The greater the average period between premium payment and loss payout, the greater the influence of investment returns in setting rates. Thus, investment results can be exceedingly important in annuities, long-term care insurance, and some forms of disability income insurance. They are relatively less important in group life and health insurance, in term life insurance, and in some forms of health insurance.

SECTION-3

THE HUMAN LIFE VALUE CONCEPT

The human life value (HLV) concept is a part of the general theory of human capital. Although this has been an area of inquiry for more than four centuries. Only recently the interrelationship between human capital and life insurance has been acknowledged.[4] Some resemblance of the idea is expressed in the Code of Hammurabi, the Bible, the Koran, and early Anglo-Saxon law, in which it was used to determine the compensation allowed to the relatives of an individual killed by a third party. In recent years, the valuation of a human life, in connection with legal actions seeking recovery for wrongful death has gained prominence. A considerable body of literature was developed in this area, contributing to a more scientific approach to the calculation of damages in wrongful-death cases. Whatever philosophy is adopted, we must take care to avoid confusing human life valuation with ethical concepts of worth.

Apparently, the HLV concept was first applied to life insurance in the 1880s through the efforts of Jacob L. Green, then president of the Connecticut Mutual Life Insurance Company. However, until the 1920s that the concept became established an economic basis for life and health insurance.

In contrast to human capital, which is the production potential of an individual, human life value is a measure of the actual future earnings or values of services of individual-that is the capitalized value of an individual's future net earnings after subtracting self-maintenance costs such as food, clothing, and shelter. From the standpoint of one's dependents, an individual's human life value is the measure of the value of benefits that the dependents can expect from their breadwinner or supporter. Similar from the viewpoint of an organization, the human life value of an employee is the value of his or her services to the firm. Therefore, under this approach, there is not necessarily on single human life value. A given human life value is a function of its purpose and value to others.

SECTION-4

HEALTH INSURANCE IN INDIA

Health insurance is mostly neglected subject with our insurers in India. The mediclaim policy introduced by the General Insurance Corporation has caught the attention of our people because of exclusion of many diseases and surgical intervention.

HEALTH INSURANCE AS AN ADJUNCT OF LIFE INSURANCE

It was considered by LIC in year 1993 and that too for four major diseases namely.

(i) Cancer
(ii) Paralytic Stroke leading to disability
(iii) Renal failure (both kidney)
(iv) Coronary artery diseases

TYPES OF POLICY

- Asha Deep I
- Jeevan Asha II
- Asha Deep II

It is a life insurance plan which covers the risk of four major ailments.

(i) Cancer (malignant)
(ii) Paralytic Stroke Leading to permanent disability

Some other features are

(i) Minimum age at entry 18 years
(ii) Maximum age at entry 50 years
(iii) Maximum age at maturity 65 years
(iv) Minimum sum assured Rs.50,000
(v) Maximum sum assured Rs.5,00,000
(vi) Policy terms 15, 20 and 25 years

These are the features for Asha Deep II Health Insurance Policy. It is an improvement of its earlier per Asha Deep II.

JEEVAN ASHA II

Double/Triple accident benefits: The proposer will have an option to choose an exclusive additional amount payable on death due to accident to be equal to or double the sum assured for payment of an additional annual premium of Re.1 or Rs.2 respectively per Rs.1,000 sum assured.[5]

THE MARKET FOR HEALTH INSURANCE

Health care usually involves the purchase of Health Insurance with insurance, monetary consideration of a market are not primary when health care is required. Insurance also spreads risks by providing protection against large unforeseen medical expenses.

Private Insurance Markets may not provide the means for individuals to protect themselves against the costs of adverse health for the reasons for failure of private insurance.

(1) The private market also has limitations in providing health coverage because of adverse selection, and because of exclusion of some people who cannot afford health insurance.

(2) Private Insurance companies attempt to solve adverse selection problems by denying health insurance to people with high expected health costs.

(3) The dilemmas of the choice between market and government and perhaps no where.

A substantial part of the cost of health insurance may well be paid by employees, even if employers make the payments to health insurance companies. The true burden of payment is determined by supply and demand elasticities in a market and not by who transfers the money. (p. 744).

CURRENT SCENARIO AND ISSUES IN HEALTH INSURANCE IN INDIA

Healthcare sector in India is fragmented between the centre and the states and the overall legal framework relating to the regulation of healthcare is not simple. Though the Government of India was a part to the 1978 WHO declaration (Alma Ata Declaration) and commitment of "Health for all by 2000 AD," precious little was attained by the target date.

Until 1978, 70 per cent of the hospital beds were in the public sector and in 1998, 80 per cent of the hospital beds were in the private sector. The Eighth plan recommended: "It is time that the concept of free medical care is reviewed and people are required to pay even if partially, for the services."

The draft National Health Policy-2001 (NHP-2001) commented: "The contribution of the private sector in providing health services would be much enhanced particularly for the population group which can afford to pay for services." The gradual dwindling of the role of the public sector in health care does not augur well for a country like India where a sizeable segment of the population lives below the poverty line.

Health Insurance is one of the most regulated forms of insurance business in those countries where it plays a dominant role in financing of health expenditures. Spiralling healthcare costs and rapid technological advances in the medical field have triggered the need for cost containment by the health insurers without sacrificing the interest of the policyholders or claimants. The nature of loss in health insurance might result in differences of opinion. All these call for intervention by regulatory authorities to protect the consumers.

However, under the Insurance Regulatory Development Authority (IRDA) in India, the powers of licensing and regulating insurance, including health insurance, has been mandated under an act of parliament.

India with a population of 1000 million experiences a vast inequality that exists in the healthcare industry with barely 3 per cent of the population covered by some form of health insurance, either social or private. The guiding principle of Bhore Committee in 1946 that 'no individual should fail to secure adequate medical care because of inability to pay for it' looks unreachable still, after 50 years of Indian independence.

In India, presently the health insurance exists in the form of Mediclaim policy offered to the individual or to any group, association or corporate bodies. Although, total expenditure on health in India is nearly 6 per cent of the entire GDP, the government spending is less than 25 per cent against the average spending of 30-40 per cent in other developing countries. Penetration of Mediclaim is currently done by state-owned insurance companies, covering only about 2.5 million people i.e. less than 0.50 per cent of the country's population.

Even Social Insurance Scheme available in India, such as the Employee State Insurance Scheme (ESIS) and Central Government Health Scheme (CGHS) have restricted coverage to a very small segment of the population, around 3 per cent. Therefore, the health insurance policy in India is nothing but a burden of inefficiency of government run system.[6]

Health insurance in India, whether publicly or privately financed, covers a small segment of the population. There is considerable support for broader health insurance coverage, including expanding the role of private health insurance. This view is part of the Health Strategy of the GOI, which included among its goals recognition of the importance of further development of private sector and of private health insurance specifically. Table 1 depicts the current coverage of the Indian population by selected health insurance schemes (Note: Data collection is not systematic and sources have not been verified).

There are numerous ways that countries around the world have attempted to broaden health insurance and specifically private health insurance. One of the more unusual methods taking shape in India is through the work of the Insurance Regulatory and Development Authority (IRDA).

Table 1
Selected Health Coverage in India

Source of Coverage	*Covered Lives (Thousands)*
Central Government Health Scheme	4,26
Mediclaim	10,000
Universal Health Insurance Scheme	Not available
ESI	31,050
Government Non-Life Insurance Companies	56
Non-Government Non-Life Insurance Companies	13
Employer Sponsored	30,000

1. Ministry of Health, 2. Express Healthcare Management, March 1-15, 2004, 3. ESIS Corporation, 4. Data submitted to IRDA, October 2003, 5. Express Healthcare Management, March 1-15, 2004.

India spends about 5 per cent of GDP for health care, which is below the average for low to middle-income countries. The GOI reports that public spending on health dropped precipitously during the decade of the 1990's, to under 1 per cent of GDP by 1999, lower than all but 5 countries in the world. There is evidence that the limited amount the government does spend is spent disproportionately on those with higher incomes (this is due, in part, to the decentralized public financing to State government, with wealthier states being able to spend more on health than poorer states.[7]

The following strategies can be suggested to overcome obstacles in the development and regulation of health insurance in India.

- Perspective of Business, Consumers, and Providers
- Legal and Regulatory
- Consumer Information and Activism

India's one billion citizens pay for over four-fifths of health care expenditures out-of pocket. A more developed health insurance market could both protect citizens and permit the public sector to focus its limited resources on the most vulnerable.

"Health insurance properly developed and regulated can act as a bridge between patients and providers balancing quality care at reasonable costs with and effective and accountable health care."[8]

NEW SCHEMES AND NEW PLAYER

Insurance schemes that can cater to the different segments of the population should be introduced and encouraged. The schemes could vary on the basis of differences in the provider networks chosen and (for example) the length of stay or cost permitted per procedure. These schemes could be launched by the insurance companies or by any one of the several healthcare providers. The Health Status in India has been analysed with the help of the following Tables (Ref. 2, 3, 4 and 5). These tables are self explanatory in nature.

Table 2
Selected Socio-Economic Indicators, 2000-2001

Sl.N.	*Item of Information*	*Reference Period and Data*		
1.	Age distribution of population %	**1971**	**1981**	**1991**
	0-14	42.0	39.6	37.8
	15-59	52.0	53.9	55.5
	60+	6.0	6.5	6.7
		1941-51	**1991**	**2000**
2.	Crude Birth Rate (SRS) per thousand	27.4	9.8#	8.5
3.	Crude Death Rate (SRS) per thousand	27.4	9.8#	8.5
4.	General Fertility Rate (SRS)	**1981**	**1990**	**1999**
	Rural	149.4	132.6	112.8
	Urban	107.2	96.1	77.6
	Total	140.9	123.9	103.2
5.	Total Fertility Rate	**1981**	**1990**	**1999**
	Rural	4.8	4.1	3.5
	Urban	3.3	2.8	2.3
	Total	4.5	3.8	3.2
6.	Expectation of life at birth (years)	**1947**	**1986-91**	**2001-06**
	Persons	31.7	58.6	64.8
	Male	32.0	58.1	64.1
	Female	31.4	59.1	65.8
7.	No. of Hospital	1952	1982	1999
		2694	6804	15500
8.	Beds per lakh population	32	83	93
9.	No. of Primary Health Centres	4793	20139	22842
10.	No. of Community Health Centres	–	2070	3043
11.	No. of Doctors per lakh population	17	47	56
12.	No. of Dentist per million population	9	13	39

Source: Statistical Abstract India, 2002.

Table 3
India: Regulatory Status of Selected Health Care Financing Schemes

Health Financing Schemes	*Legal Regimes*	*Regulator*
Private Commercial Health Insurance	Commercial law, Insurance Act 1938 and IRDA Act 1999 and regulations	IRDA
Public Sector Insurance Companies (A) Commercial Competitive (B) Subsidized non-competitive	Own Acts; and Insurance Act 1938	(a) IRDA (b) Central Govt., Ministry of Finance (Subsidies)
ESIS	Own Act	Ministry of labour
Corporate self health insurance	Commercial law	Unregulated
Community-based health insurance	Associations law, cooperatives law	Unregulated. Subsidies by the Ministry of Finance entail hidden regulation
Exempted schemes (Calcutta Hospital and Nursing Home Benefit Association)	Own legal status not affected by the Insurance Nationalization Act	IRDA

Table 4
Selected Health Indicators

(Persons at Years)

Sl. No.	*Parameters*	*1951*	*1981*	*1991*	*Current Level*
1.	Crude Birth Rate (per 1000 Population)	40.8	33.9	29.5	25.0 (2002*)
2.	Crude Death Rate	25.1	12.5	9.8	81 (2002*)
3.	Total Fertility Rate (TFR)	6.0	4.5	3.6	3.2 (1999)
4.	Maternal Mortality (MMR) (Per 10,000 live births) NFHS	N.A	N.A	437	407 (1998)
5.	Infant Mortality Rate (Per 1000 live births)	146 (1951-61)	110	80	64 (2002*)
6.	Child (0-4 years) Mortality Rate Per 1000 Children	57.3 (1972)	41.2	26.5	19.5 (2000)
7.	Couple Protection Rate (per cent)	10.4 (1971)	22.8	44.1	48.2 (1998-9)
8.	Life Expectancy at Birth Male	37.2	54.1	59.7 (1991-95)	63.9 (2001-06)
	Female	36.2	54.7	60.9 (1991-95)	66.9 (2001-06)

Note: The dates in the brackets indicate years for which latest information is available.
NFHS: National Family Health Survey, *N.A:* Not Available *Provisional

Source: Economic Survey 2003-2004.

Table 5
Population Projections (millions)

Year	*2000*	*2005*	*2010*	*2015*	*2020*
Total	1,010	1,093	1,175	1,256	1,331
Under 15	631	368	370	372	373
15-64	604	673	747	819	882
65+	45	51	58	65	76

Source: Report of India Vision 2020 Committee Planning Commission.

Health insurance or quasi health insurance schemes operated by all entities including NGOs, would, however, need to be registered with the IRDA and, therefore, regulated and monitored by it. The IRDA could lay down a threshold number of members above which a scheme would have to be registered with it even if it is not offered through an insurance company.

There is a need for one comprehensive insurance product that takes care of all health insurance requirements of the insured.

ONGOING INITIATIVES BY STATES FOR HEALTH INSURANCE

- For Meeting hospitalization cost of BPI family. Kerala has proposed a Health Insurance Scheme with contribution from the individual, State and PRI administered through Kutumbashree self-help group.
- In Delhi, a government funded health insurance scheme 'Arogya Nidhi' is being taken up. For secondary care in government institutions, the state plans to initiate a pilot project on health insurance for people below the poverty line.
- In Andhra Pradesh a health insurance scheme is being implemented, under which a cover of Rs. 20,000 towards hospitalization charges for a period of five years is assured for the acceptor of sterilization and his/her two children, subject to a maximum of Rs. 4,000 per year.
- Madhya Pradesh and Himachal Pradesh are in the process of launching Community Health Insurance Schemes.[9]

Health insurance is one of the most regulated forms of insurance business in countries where it plays a dominant role in healthcare financing of health expenditures. An exhaustive range of health insurance regulations that address to the needs of growing healthcare financing complexities would be necessary.

REASONS FOR INTRODUCING HEALTH INSURANCE IN INDIA

1. It is being increasingly realized that even low-income groups can make small periodic contributions, which can add up to a significant

amount, thereby taking some pressure off from already strained state revenues.

2. The insured people would have the options of going to either a public or private service provider, which in turn would generate competition among providers for better services.
3. Health insurance can be used to promote certain desirable behaviour. For example, Aarogya Raksha scheme of Andhra Pradesh links family planning to health insurance.[10]

COMMUNITY BASED UNIVERSAL HEALTH INSURANCE SCHEME

Prior to the recent announcement of the proposed community based universal health insurance scheme by the finance minister of India, various state governments were contemplating launching health insurance scheme for the poor population. State governments intensified their efforts when a similar announcement by the central government a year ago (in the budget of 2002-03), did not take off. Without a sufficient knowledge base, state governments were trying to enter into an arrangement with the providers of medical services, public insurance companies and the target community, whereby insurance companies would reimburse treatment costs of the target community and governments would subsidise the premium for the insurance sold to the target community. Some state governments had thought of paying the premium through their general revenues while others had planned to cross-subsidise it by bringing state government employees under a Mediclaim policy (Punjab and West Bengal Governments alone were thinking on these lines). With the announcement (in the budget of 2003-04) made by the then finance minister to launch community based universal health insurance scheme for the low-income population, state governments have put off their plans. The Inter state variation in Performance of Universal Health Insurance Scheme in quite evident from Table 6.

Before analyzing the scheme that was launched, let us first look at some of its important features. The scheme comes in three different types: (i) Re 1 per day per year for an individual (ii) Rs. 1.5 per day per year for a family of up to five members and (iii) Rs. 2 per day per year for a family enrolment, as opposed to individual, enrolment is obvious. What are the benefits provided? Well, in case of hospitalization the scheme provides medical expenses up to Rs. 30,000 per family, if an earning member falls sick the scheme also provides for the loss of livelihood at the rate of Rs. 50 per day up to a maximum of 15 days, and in case of death of the earning head of the family due to personal accident, Rs. 25,000 is given to the nominee.

Table 6
Interstate Variation in Performance of Universal Health Insurance Scheme

State	*Total No. of Families in UHI Scheme*	*Beds per 1,00,000 of Popn**	*Popn in 1,00,000 2001*	*Per cent of BPL*	*Families Insured per 1,00,000 of Popn*
A	*B*	*C*	*D*	*E*	*F=B/D*
Andhra Pradesh	41656	68.91	757.27	15.77	55.01
Assam	15711	56.49	266.38	36.06	58.98
Bihar	3456	33.68	828.78	42.60	4.17
Gujarat	28290	153.51	505.96	14.07	74.68
Haryana	8176	43.61	210.82	8.74	38.78
Himachal Pradesh	1610	98.01	60.77	7.63	26.49
Karnataka	19982	85.49	527.33	20.04	37.89
Kerala	35021	265.3	318.38	12.72	110.00
Madhya Pradesh	15378	27.41	603.85	37.43	25.47
Maharashtra	87494	99.98	967.52	25.02	90.43
Orissa	3041	47.01	367.06	47.15	8.28
Punjab	24617	73.07	242.89	6.16	101.35
Rajasthan	38113	48.15	564.73	15.28	67.49
Tamil Nadu	39933	87.33	621.1	21.12	64.49
Uttar Pradesh	20017	33.99	1660.52	31.15	12.05
West Bengal	4070	81.13	802.21	27.02	2.07
Total	396565		9305.57		

Note: *India Health Report, Oxford University Press, 2003, *Source:* Date on insurance provided by General Insurance Public Sector Association (GIPSA), Poverty figures capture percentage of population below poverty line (NSSO 55th Round)

Source: *Economic and Political Weekly*, October 9-15, 2004.

PROBLEMS FACING THE HEALTH CARE INDUSTRY

The most important impediments arise from the supply side, i.e., from the health care providers. Lack of standards for diseases and treatment procedures (where these standards and procedures exist, their adoption is lacking); absence of rating and credentialing of providers; non-existence of a centralized database, lack of standardized billing, claims and proposal forms are some of the problems facing the health care industry.

PRIVATE HEALTH INSURANCE IN INDIA

Although a number of private insurance companies have entered after the liberalization of the insurance market in 2000, no significant change in health insurance has been observed either in terms of new health insurance products or in terms of the volume of business. The two health insurance products, namely, Mediclaim for the general public and Jan Arogya for the poor, launched prior to the liberalization, have not shown any significant growth either in terms of volume of business or in the number of policies sold post-liberalisation. See Tables 7 and 8.

Table 7
Mediclaim Policy

	1997-98	*1998-99*	*1999-2000*	*2000-01*	*2001-02*
No of persons insured	2783862.0	3534417.0	4894129.0	5623864.0	7784491.0
Premium (Rs. in lakhs)	21569.6	27173.5	38040.7	51898.2	74204.5
Claims (Rs. in lakhs)	18612.4	21810.3	33226.1	47152.8	62038.6
Claims ratio (per cent)	86.3	80.3	87.3	90.9	83.6

Source: Annual Reports of the (Non-life) Public Insurance Companies.

Table 8
Jan Arogya Bima Policy

	1997-98	*1998-99*	*1999-2000*	*2000-01*	*2001-02*
No of persons insured	139354.0	313643.0	686685.0	348413.0	348912.0
Premium (Rs. In lakhs)	115.3	2880.3	6569.0	6800.3	9097.3
Claims (Rs in lakhs)	97.1	2882.4	7978.0	6689.0	8818.2
Claims ratio (per cent)	84.3	100.1	121.4	98.4	97.4

Source: Annual Reports of the (Non-life) Public Insurance Companies.

SECTION–5

CONCLUSION

The Health Insurance business in India will continue to evolve. Infact, change in insurance is occurring at an unprecedented pace. At the same time, the fundamentals of rist and insurance however, do not change. We have understood that economies as a great discipline using as an indispensable tool to evolve a theoretical paradigm in order to explain the problems in the area of health insurance. Health Insurance is also a good device under Social Security measures. That is the reason why the Government of India had come forward to introduce the Universal Health Insurance Scheme in the year 2003.

This paper has also highlighted the problem of interstate variation in the performance of Universal Health Insurance Scheme in India with adequate secondary level data. Experience shows that, the study of health insurance is mostly neglected subject of research in the Indian context.

A close examination of the data on health status in India reveals that, India has to go further, in order to have satisfactory level in the avenue of health insurance. Health insurance is emerging as an important financing tool in meeting the health care needs of the poor. The increased public health spending and revamping of public health facilities is a must for the success of the Community Based Health Insurance Scheme.

Notes and Reference

1. Gary S. Becker (1962), "Investment in Human Capital: A Theoretical Analysis", *The Journal of Political Economy,* Vol. 70, (October 1962) pp. 9-49.
2. Harold D. Skipper Jr. (1988), *"Rationale for Government Intervention into Insurance Markets"*, in Harold D Skipper Jr., ed., International Risk and Insurance: An Environmental - Managerial Approach (Boston: Irwin Mc Graw-Hil, 1988) pp. 243-254.
3. David F. Babbel (1985), "The Price Elasticity of Demand for Whole Life Insurance", *The Journal of Finance* (March 1985), pp. 225-239.
4. Alfred E. Hofflander (1996), "The Human Life Value: An Historical Perspective", *The Journal of Risk and Insurance,* Vol. 33, (September 1996), pp. 381-391.
5. Ganguly Anand (2002), *"Insurance Management,"* New Age International Publishers.
6. Banerjee Deepanjan, Health Insurance in India–Time for Conscious Revolution, *www.healthnsurancerevolution.htm.*
7. Chaturvedi H., Dharmendra Kumar and Rahul Singh (2005), (ed.), *India Insurance Report, Series I,* Allied Publishers, Birla Institute of Management Technology.
8. Srinivasan R. (2001), *Health and Population Perspectives and Issues,* April June, 24(2), 65-72.
9. *Economic Survey,* Government of India, 2004.
10. Ahuja Rajeev (2004), Health Insurance for the Poor, *Economic and Political Weekly,* July 10-16, 2004, Vol. XXXIX, No. 28, pp. 3171-77.

Is India Facing a Recession or a Slowdown of Growth

GANESH L.*

INTRODUCTION

There is a subdued optimism over the growth prospects for the Indian economy even in the face of such extraordinary turmoil. It is true that along with the rest of the world, India's performance will not match its recent record. The slowdown will affect the economy but at the end of the day there would be evidence of solid growth.

Financial Crisis : Industrial Sector

It is a challenge to forecast India's GDP growth because of its extremely difficult economic environment. On Feb 9th 2009, the CSO in its advance estimate placed India's GDP growth for the current year at 7.1 per cent (*The Hindu*, Feb. 16 2009). Earlier in November it had estimated the growth during the first half (April-September) at 7.8%, hence as per advance estimates it should be 6.4% for the second half. Figures for Oct-Dec. 2008 have not yet been released but all available data point to a decreasing figure. Monthly figures of exports during this quarter show a negative growth. The IIP (Index of Industrial Production) numbers clearly indicate the strain which the manufacturing sector is now facing. For the first time since April 1993, figures show the industrial growth has contracted by 0.04 per cent. The fear is that the IIP may continue to slide further till the end of 2009 and a recovery could only set in later. As industrial slow down would have a bearing on the country's over all GDP growth, the council would revisit the

* Assistant Professor, Christ University, Institute of Management, Bangalore-560 029, (*e-mail: ganesh.l@christuniversity.in*)

GDP growth figures, which is now at 7.7 per cent for 2008-09. Meanwhile, the Asian Development Bank (ADB) has already scaled down India's GDP growth projection to 7 per cent from the earlier estimate of 7.4 per cent for 2008 on account of the global financial crisis directly impacting the banking system and financial markets in the country. For the calendar year 2009, ADB forecast a further decline in economic growth to 6.5 per cent.

India, South Asia's most dynamic economy, in recent years is reeling from the direct effect of the global financial crisis on its banking system and financial markets. The growth projection for India has been revised down to 7 per cent in 2008 and 6.5 per cent in 2009 from 9 per cent in 2007. With over a 12 per cent development in exports, a deceleration in industrial growth during the month was expected. But to our surprise, the decline was bigger than expected which is a disappointing scenario for industrial growth. However, the IIP data shows that the production growth in two out of the four segments that make up the manufacturing index - intermediate and consumer goods - shrank to 3.7 per cent and minus 2.3 per cent from the robust growth of 13.9 and 13.7 per cent, respectively.

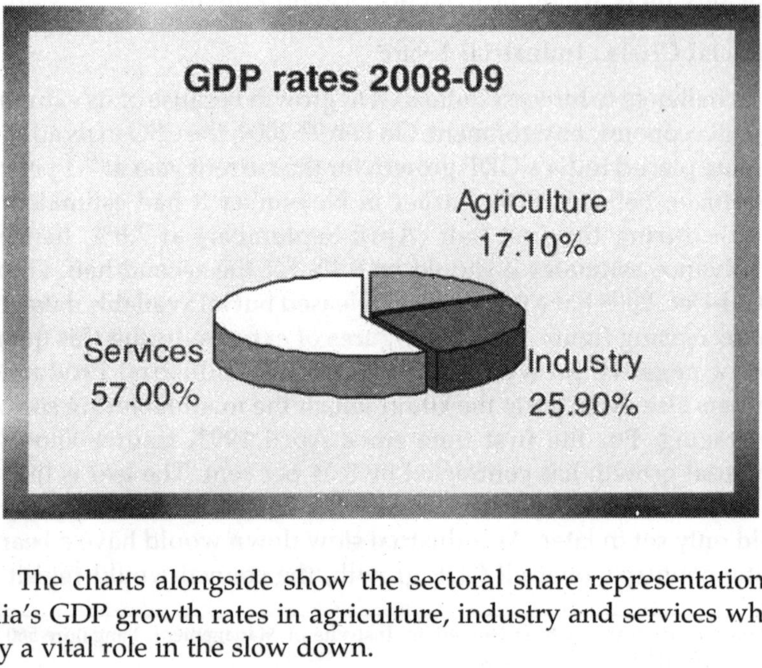

The charts alongside show the sectoral share representation of India's GDP growth rates in agriculture, industry and services which play a vital role in the slow down.

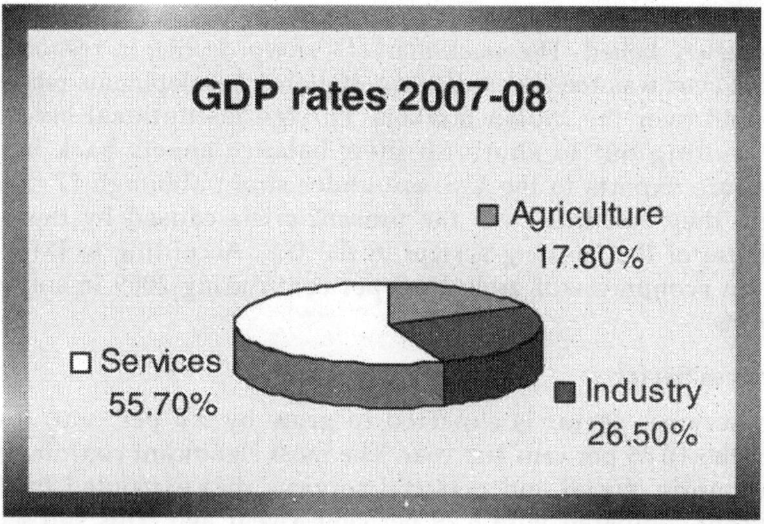

Agricultural sector

Agriculture is the major source of livelihood and employment for the people in the rural economy of the country. The slackening rate of the farm sector growth during the Tenth Plan has resulted in a drop in the sector's share. The national average growth rate in the agriculture and allied sector during the Tenth Plan was nearly 2.29% in line with the changing composition of the GDP, the contribution of agriculture to its GSDP (Gross State Domestic Product) changing because of inadequate rainfall, frequent drought and a decline in investment in the farm sector. As per the IIP, agricultural sector's share of India's GDP declined from 17.8 per cent in 2007-08 to 17.1 per cent in 2008-09. Although the farm sector's share in GSDP has declined, it has been at a faster pace than the reduction in the proportion of the workforce engaged in the sector. As per the population index, out of 72 per cent of the rural population, 58.3 per cent were classified as cultivators/ laborers. This distress in agriculture is causing farmers to migrate to urban areas looking for employment to compensate for the lack of opportunities and low growth in rural incomes. The major challenge is the rejuvenation of agriculture so that agriculture becomes a viable, sustainable and an eco friendly source of income.

Software Exports

Remittances and earnings from software exports that had propped up the current account in the past, shows signs of decline. Expectations that India's economy is decoupled from the west have been completely belied. The stock market's sharp decline in response to global cues was the first indication of global developments retaining its hold over the Indian markets. Foreign institutional investors are pulling out to shore up their balance sheets back home. Software exports to the U.S. are under strain although IT majors think they can tide over the present crisis caused by the near collapse of the banking system in the U.S. According to IMF, the Indian economy will grow by 5 per cent during 2009 in software exports.

Services Sector

The services sector is expected to grow by 9.6 per cent, lower than the 10.85 per cent last year. The most significant contributor is community, social and personal services that expanded by 9.28 per cent compared with 6.79 per cent a year ago. This sub sector has the potential to grow even more as it captures government expenditure, including the sixth pay commission award, the stimulus packages and grants for expenditure approved in October 2008. Indian salaries were rising compared to other countries. The companies which are likely to be affected the most are those which are servicing the financial institutions in the advanced countries that have been facing a slow down. These institutions can easily come up. Present position of unemployment among the technically trained people *is due to a decline in outsourcing* for a while. Hence in the services sector also it is a slow down in growth and not a recession.

RBI to Revise GDP estimates

During October, RBI had made certain announcements in the midterm monetary policy review. It has estimated the 2008-09 growth rates at 7.5-8 per cent with a downside bias. After a re-look, the IMF reduced the 2008 global growth rates from 3.9 per cent to 3.2 per cent while reducing 2009 figure from 3.7 per cent to 2.2 per cent. For emerging economies, the GDP growth rate was brought down from6.1 per cent to 5.1 per cent. A similar trend of lowering the growth forecast is seen among professional forecasters in India. According to the RBI which publishes these data ahead of the quarterly credit policy statement, the median forecast of professional forecasters was 8.1 per cent in April. It came down to 7.9 per cent in July and to 7.7 per cent in Oct and then to 6.8 per cent in Jan. 2009.

SUMMARY AND CONCLUSION

The meltdown is financial in nature and it has an impact on the financial institutions in the advanced industrial countries. This, in turn has an impact on the real economy leading to recession. India will essentially influence the demand for its exports and capital inflows, which will get affected through the balance of payments mechanism. As for banks, their exposure to these kinds of toxic instruments has been negligible. They are adequately capitalized, an advantage derived from the fact that they are owned by the government. Hence financial institutions are in good shape. There is an irrational unwillingness on the part of the banks to lend, which is slowing down the economy. First, the government has to work out the sectoral packages for the affected industries contributing to exports and next must attract inflows by relaxing restrictions on the external commercial borrowings basically to induce NRI deposits. High foreign exchange reserves have, in the current global recession, saved Asian countries during the financial crisis of 1997-2000. But if savings and forex reserves are high in Asia, there is a chance for the Americans and Europeans to do so; then the world demand will collapse and the slowdown would become a recession and the end would be depression. Saving too much can be as harmful as saving too little.

As per current scenario, India is facing only a slow down and not a recession. Policy makers are desperately trying to fix their financial sectors so as not to enter into a depression. However the present positions are a big stress faced by the micro and small enterprises, exports, the IT and steel sectors.

Microfinance and Disaster Management: An Institutional Approach

R. KUMAR* AND K. SAMBASIVAM**

INTRODUCTION

Phnom Penh, the capital of Cambodia, experiences an annual flood every year during September/October, when monsoon rains to the north swell the rivers of the lower Mekong delta. For many, the high waters are a refreshing sight, as they signal cooler weather to come. They also help to flush out the river systems, and the silt deposited on the flood plains helps to keep the soil fertile. The annual flood is, for many, a potent symbol of life and renewal. It is not a "disaster" but an "event". Many of the city's poorest people live in slum communities to the south-east of the city, along the banks of the *Tonle Bassac.* One such community is a commune called *Chbar Ampeou,* which literally means "Sugarcane Garden". At one time it would have been a perfect place to grow sugarcane, as the soil is rich and moist thanks to the annual inundation. However, *Chbar Ampeou* is now home to many thousands of Phnom Penh's poorest households. The poorest tend to live closer to the river and lower down, as rent is generally proportional to distance from the riverbank. With an average income of less than $1 per day, 50 per cent of children malnourished, few children attending school, domestic violence rife, many women forced to survive through prostitution, an AIDS epidemic, and no sanitation services, this community is a microcosm of failed Millennium Development Goals!

For many people of *Chbar Ampeou,* the annual flood is a severe hindrance. The paths leading to their homes are covered by water,

* Lecturer in Economics (SS) DDE, Annamalai University.
** Lecturer in Economics (SG), Bharathidasan Govt. College for Women, Pondicherry 605 003.

sometimes metres deep. They have to construct narrow plank walkways to give access to their homes. It becomes so much harder for people to get to their places of work, and some have to relocate their shops or stalls. Any belongings stored at lower levels need to be lifted higher. Small children are at constant risk of drowning. When the river slows the water stagnates and becomes so toxic that it is a very serious health hazard. All of this adds to the already high relative cost of living for these households. Nevertheless, these longsuffering people have learned to cope with it, one way or another. In financial terms, these households employ a number of tactics to cope with the extra demands of flood season. Many households consume less, reducing their food intake significantly. They liquidate savings they might have accumulated, either by selling physical items or withdrawing cash if they were one of the few people fortunate enough to have access to cash deposit services. Some seek loans from various informal sources or from the microfinance initiatives of NGOs. Some default on repayments of existing loans. Others are forced to sell productive assets.

In September 2000, the rains were heavier than usual and the river swelled to its highest level in many decades. Many homes in *Chbar Ampeou* were completely submerged, some collapsed, and it was too dangerous to remain in those dwellings that remained. Thousands of people were rendered homeless and all personal belongings except those they could carry were lost. With the assistance of Disaster Management agencies (DMAs), they were able to set up temporary shelters along roadsides or in local *Wats*. A cholera epidemic added to their woes. The physical, mental and financial stress faced by many of these families lasted many months and for some, there was no recovery. Natural disasters such as those caused by flood, storm, earthquake, tidal waves, fire, etc. are a harsh fact of life for many poor households and therefore, for the microfinance institutions (MFIs) that target them. The current literature on "Microfinance and Natural Disasters" tends to focus on relief and reconstruction activities (including non-financial and financial services) that immediately follow a natural disaster. However, disaster management is much more than this. It includes pre-disaster activities such as risk mitigation and early warning systems, as well as long-term post-disaster rehabilitation. This paper argues that there are numerous opportunities for collaboration between MFIs and DMAs that go beyond emergency relief and reconstruction. This collaboration can be mutually reinforcing, allowing MFIs and DMAs to concentrate on their core competencies and to leverage their particular expertise for the ultimate benefit of their clients - poor households that are particularly vulnerable to natural disasters.

MICROFINANCE AND DISASTER MANAGEMENT

Microfinance is the provision of relevant and affordable financial services to poor households that do not have access to the services offered by 'traditional' financial institutions. The 'micro' prefix refers to the size of the financial transactions; it does not imply that the MFIs themselves are small. Microfinance is primarily concerned with credit and savings although, in recent times, allied services such as insurance, leasing, payment transfers and remittances are being introduced to the mix of services. Demand for microfinance services usually comes from 'micro entrepreneurs'; people who survive by generating income for themselves in very small business activities. Providing microfinance services to poor clients requires innovative operating methods to manage risk and reduce transaction costs. Poor households do not usually have physical assets to offer as collateral for loans, so microfinance providers have developed substitutes. The most common form of substitute collateral has been the formation of groups of borrowers and the establishment of joint-liability procedures, where loan group members effectively guarantee one another's loans. To reduce transaction costs, microfinance providers primarily deal with these loan groups rather than with individual clients and they outsource various administration tasks to the groups.

Some MFIs have developed from existing community-based savings and loans cooperatives. In India, for example, these are often referred to as village "self-help" groups. Other MFIs have evolved out of the revolving loan programs of charitable non-government organisations, which offered loans to help beneficiaries develop income-generating activities. Other MFIs have been established by commercial banks or government-owned development banks, either as a response to their observation that providing financial services to the poor could be a suitably viable business opportunity, or as a response to government edict that they provide financial services to all segments of the community, including the poor.

Since the early 1990s, a major emphasis within the microfinance sector has been on institutional development, including building the quality and capacity of the governance and management of MFIs. This institutional development is necessary for a number of reasons. First, if MFIs accept client deposits, they are generally required to meet the prudential and regulatory requirements as defined in local banking laws. Essentially, they are required to become licensed banks. Second, institutional maturity is needed to enable growth in client outreach. Growth in the client base allows the MFI to reap advantages of scale, thereby achieving a greater degree of financial sustainability. (Financial sustainability for an MFI means that it is generating enough revenue from interest charges and fees to cover all direct and indirect costs, including operating expenses, provision for loan losses, and adjusted cost of capital). Third, institutional maturity is necessary to attract capital investment, whether concessionary or commercial, from external sources. The overriding mission of an MFI is to provide financial services to poor households on a sustainable basis. While most MFIs have a pro-poor, development-oriented emphasis, they are more correctly understood as banks rather than as charitable development organisations. Indeed, many MFIs are licensed banks.

Natural Disasters, Disaster Mitigation and Disaster Management

A *Natural Disaster* is "a natural event, sudden or progressive, with such severity that the affected community or country has to respond by taking exceptional measures".

Disaster Mitigation is "measures aimed at reducing the impact of a natural or man-made disaster on the nation or community; and the application of these measures to moderate or reduce the effects and impacts of current or future disasters".

Disaster Management is "an applied science that seeks by systematic observation and analysis of disasters, to improve measures relating to prevention, mitigation, preparedness, emergency response and recovery".(Silver, 2001) Severe natural events include flood, cyclone (or typhoon/hurricane), fire, blizzard, earthquake, tsunami, volcanic eruption, etc. Some of these are "rapid-onset", some are "slow-onset", some are seasonal, some are predictable, and some are restricted to specific geographic areas.

Disaster management is a complicated, on-going concern, involving far more than the immediate distribution of emergency relief in the wake of a natural disaster. There is a cycle of activities that are in progress long before a natural disaster strikes and continue long after the causal event has passed. It is important to note that use of the term "disaster" is not an indication of the severity of a natural event but of the severity of its impact on people and the environment. Therefore, all aspects of disaster management including mitigation and preparedness, emergency response, rehabilitation and reconstruction can all serve to reduce the impact of a severe natural event.

While natural events are indiscriminate, their impact is usually more devastating for poor households because they have fewer options for coping with them. Poor households are also more likely to be located in "danger" zones, for example, below the flood line. This is why natural disasters appear to strike the poor more often - because, in fact, they do. Most recent discussions regarding "Microfinance and Natural Disasters" focus primarily on the relatively short period of immediate emergency relief. This is understandable because the period immediate following a severe natural event is often a point of "discontinuity" for microfinance activities, requiring specific measures. This paper, however, also addresses some broader issues of "Microfinance and Disaster Management", in recognition of the need for MFIs to take a more responsive (and less reactive) approach to disaster management and mitigation. There are numerous opportunities for collaboration between MFIs and DMAs that go beyond emergency relief activities to pre-disaster risk mitigation, longer-term post-disaster rehabilitation, and disaster research. This collaboration can be mutually reinforcing, allowing MFIs and DMAs to concentrate on their core competencies and to maximise the efficacy of their interventions.

ECONOMIC IMPACT OF NATURAL DISASTERS

The impact of a natural disaster is rarely uniform across all households in a community or region, and the specific impacts depend on the nature of the disaster. Nevertheless, natural disasters typically impact the finances of poor households in a number of ways. First, the disaster might affect the household's ability to earn income. It might be difficult or impossible for income-earners to reach their customers or for customers to reach them. There might be reduced demand for the products or services that the household offers. Trading stock might have been destroyed and replacement stock might not be immediately available. Even if replacement stock is available, the household might not have funds to purchase it.

Second, poor households might face increased expenditure. Prices of essential commodities such as food or fuel might have increased dramatically due to high demand and/or short supply. Health crises or epidemics are common features of post-disaster environments and this may result in increased expenditure for health care. Also, if income-earners are injured or become sick, it might not be possible to work. Similarly, income-earners might need to take time out to care for the sick or injured. Children may be taken from school to do this. Third, the disaster might have caused damage to, or destruction of, income-generating assets such as crops, livestock, tools-of-trade or other equipment. Loss of productive assets can have a long-term impact on the ability of the household to generate income if the household does not have funds to replace these assets. Finally, the disaster might have caused damage to, or destruction of, household assets. The household might be faced with significant expenditure to replace household necessities.

The Economic Coping Mechanisms of Poor Households

Following a natural disaster, poor households will make adjustments to cope economically. "Low-stress" strategies include ceasing regular saving, reducing consumption, short-term migration of one or more family members for the purpose of obtaining paid labour, and calling in debts from neighbours and relatives. "Mediumstress" strategies include using up savings, selling non-essential household assets and obtaining loans. "Highstress" strategies include selling productive assets and loan default. The difference between these strategies is that low-stress strategies are easily reversed whereas high-stress strategies are difficult to reverse. To protect their long-term economic position, poor households need to avoid high-stress coping strategies.

There are limits to the low and medium-stress adjustments a household can make. Reduced consumption over long periods can negatively impact physical health and this can affect earning capacity. Migration of family members can be disruptive and result in a less coherent family unit. Even if a household has debts to call in, it is often the case that their debtors are facing similar hardships and might not be able to repay. Medium-stress adjustments are not always easy either. Typically, poor households will "deposit" savings by investing in physical items that might be difficult to liquidate in a time of emergency need. Markets are distorted in the wake of a natural disaster: the trade of essential commodities favours sellers whereas for non-essential items the balance is firmly in favour of buyers. Finally, loans obtained from informal sources are likely to be even more expensive than usual.

The Impact of Natural Disasters on MFIs

Given that the clients of MFIs are the poor households described above, it is common for MFIs to be impacted financially as well. First, there will be an immediate decline in inflow of cash. Clients are likely to stop depositing savings and they may opt to reduce loan repayments to the minimum required. Second, there will be an increase in outflow of cash. Clients are likely to withdraw savings and they may request additional loans.

Note that each of these actions is one of the low or medium-stress coping strategies described above and, from the client's point-of-view, they are entirely sensible (and necessary) actions to take. In the medium term, there may be a significant loss of capital if large numbers of clients are forced into loan default. Furthermore, while group-lending methodologies can ensure high repayment rates under normal conditions they can also serve to magnify capital losses in times of widespread economic stress. The result of all of the above is that MFIs may face a liquidity crisis in the wake of a natural disaster. Since MFIs pride themselves on their ability to deliver financial services to poor households, it would be both ironic and unfortunate if an MFI was unable to maintain these services at a time when their clients need them most.

The Role of MFIs in Disaster Relief

Most MFIs cannot ignore the possibility of being impacted by natural disasters. Many operate in communities and regions where severe natural events are seasonal and, to some extent, predictable. It behoves such an MFI to make preparations for the impact of natural disasters on their clients and on the MFI. Even if a natural disaster never occurs, many MFI clients will face their own "personal" disasters at some stage, and many of the strategies outlined in this paper would be beneficial to these clients in overcoming their financial difficulties. Regarding the role of MFIs in emergency relief, one debate revolves around whether MFIs should engage in general (non-financial) disaster relief activities, or whether they should concentrate on providing financial services that support clients to manage their household finances through the difficult post-disaster period. At stake is the good standing of the MFI in the diaster-affected community. On the one hand, the MFI wants to protect its identity as a member of the community that gives priority to the needs of its clients. On the other hand, the MFI wants to protect its identity as a long-term, professional financial intermediary as distinct from charitable aid organisations. There is a creative tension that it not easy to resolve, especially in the context of human suffering in the wake of a natural disaster. The argument presented in this paper is that MFIs will be better placed to respond effectively when a disaster strikes if it has worked through the issues, designed policies and products, and negotiated collaboration with DMAs, *before* disaster strikes rather than in the midst of it.

In September 2003, FDC and World Vision International conducted a workshop in Hyderabad, India entitled "Microfinance and Disaster Management". The workshop brought together 27 microfinance and disaster management practitioners from eight countries in Asia. Seven microfinance initiatives, at various stages of institutionalisation, were represented. Each one of these MFIs operates in areas where natural disasters are a regular fact of life. The policies and strategies discussed in this paper are an output of the workshop. The author acknowledges the inputs and contributions of each one of the workshop participants that informed and/or confirmed much of what is written here.

Collaboration between MFIs and DMAs

Disaster management and microfinance are specialised fields and, as such, it is important that there remains clear demarcation between the activities of each. There are, however, numerous opportunities for strategic collaboration that are mutually reinforcing, allowing MFIs and DMAs to concentrate on their core competencies and to leverage their particular expertise for the ultimate benefit of affected communities.

Disaster Preparedness

With the assistance of DMAs, MFIs should develop a disaster management plan and integrate it with existing disaster management arrangements. Where possible, MFIs should formalise relationships with DMAs and negotiate a Memorandum of Understanding with them. MFIs and DMAs should ensure that, with respect to early warning systems, two-way lines of communication are clearly defined and open. Furthermore, there should be a clearly defined external communication strategy to ensure that communities and clients receive early warnings. With the assistance of DMAs, MFIs should conduct risk mapping to better understand the vulnerability of communities to natural disasters and to reduce risk to the MFI through the geographic diversification of clientele. Similarly, MFIs should facilitate an external risk assessment of its office, its physical assets, and especially its client records. It is helpful if MFI personnel are aware of the basic principles and practices of disaster management and of the disaster relief plans that are in place for the areas in which they work. DMAs can be invited to deliver awareness-raising workshops for this purpose. Similarly, it might be helpful if relevant DMA personnel are aware of the MFI's policies for disaster-related financial products and services that might be offered following a natural disaster. MFI personnel can offer to deliver awareness-raising workshops for this purpose.

Emergency Relief

Under the direction of DMAs, the MFI and its field staff are part of the overall relief effort. Nevertheless, the priority of the MFI is the economic needs of communities, and the initial focus is on its existing clients.

MFIs should never provide cash grants. Wherever the community has access to in-kind grants from Government or other agencies, due to the disaster situation, the MFI can enable the community to obtain and share these resources.

Post-disaster Rehabilitation

With DMAs, MFI personnel may be involved in detailed disaster assessment activities (e.g. livelihood analysis, asset loss, psychological study, design of innovative products, etc.). The MFI's primary focus is on assessment of its existing clients. As the focus of disaster response moves from emergency relief to rehabilitation, the MFI needs to re-orient both its personnel and its clients, and to disengage from emergency response activities and to focus on rehabilitation.

Disaster-related Financial Products and Services

The following policies can be regarded as "good practices" for microfinance in the wake of a natural disaster. Details need to be developed for each specific context. In the interests of transparency, these policies should be communicated to clients when loans are provided and included in loan contracts.

Savings

Households that have accumulated cash savings will be better placed to cope financially following a natural disaster. Many MFIs, however, are not able to accept deposits from the general public because they are not licensed to do so. Furthermore, some MFIs decide that they will not offer deposit services, irrespective of their legal position, because this adds a level of prudential complexity and cost which they do not wish to accept. Whether they collect deposits themselves or not, MFIs should encourage their clients to accumulate savings as a buffer against disaster events. They might achieve this by educating clients about the advantages of accumulating savings, designing and applying incentives, and providing an effective savings service, for example, by employing a peripatetic deposit taker. Savings must be available for withdrawal at disaster times.

Loan Measures

As a general rule, MFIs should not make "blanket" changes to the structure of loan products following a natural disaster. However, it will sometimes be advantageous to offer temporary concessions, as it is better to forgo some income for the sake of maintaining the goodwill of clients and protecting against loan default. However, MFIs should be wary of implementing concessions that might become a recurring general expectation. Concessions should be applied in *exceptional cases* only, such as when the region has been officially declared a "natural disaster" area by an authority external to the MFI.

MFIs should try to keep its response reasonably simple, otherwise it may be difficult and costly to administer. Following are examples of the type of concessions and products that an MFI might offer. Normally, the MFI would not employ every one of these options.

As a general rule, MFIs should expect continuing full repayment. However, in some instances, it will be appropriate to offer options for temporarily reducing repayments. Repayments might be made "interest only", or they might be suspended completely for a period. MFI personnel should consider loans for rescheduling on a case-by-case basis (by individual or group). The decision to reschedule loan repayments should be based on a detailed assessment of the clients' temporary loss of income. The "grace" period should be specified at the time of rescheduling and clients should return to the normal repayment schedule as soon as possible. Interest accrues on the full balance of the loan during this period. Clients should be fully aware of the cost implications of rescheduling.

At the end of the grace period, the client might choose to make increased payments or lump sum catch-up payments, so that the loan can be completed as per the original schedule. Alternatively, the MFI might offer to extend the term of the loan. If this option is taken, the MFI will need to consider carefully how the loan will be treated in the loan portfolio, either as a loan in arrears or as a refinanced loan (see "Loan Portfolio Management Issues" below). MFIs might consider a temporary reduction of interest rates. However, without also reducing the requirement to repay capital, this option is usually of little significance. Emergency loans may be offered for the purpose of restoring productive assets and essential household assets. The decision to offer an emergency loan should be based on a detailed assessment of the client's asset loss. Standard cost structures should apply. An important aspect of emergency loans is that assessment and disbursement should be made at the earliest possible time. Group lending methodologies were designed to discourage borrowers from deliberate default but not to cover unforeseen disasters and tragedies. While group-lending methodologies can result in high repayment rates under normal conditions they can also serve to magnify losses in times of widespread economic stress. To reduce risk associated with this phenomenon, MFIs can design and implement "insurance" policies that reduce the impact of disasters on the group culture of the MFI (see "Insurance" below).

No Grants or Loan Cancellation

Loan cancellation is essentially the provision of cash grants to indebted clients. Writing-off loans has a number of negative impacts. First, it benefits different people to different degrees (those with larger loans receive greater benefit) and this can cause disharmony among clients. Second, experience has shown that writing off loans is likely to cause "repayment apathy" on future loans. Third, writing off many loans can cause serious decapitalisation of the loan fund. Loan cancellation should not be considered.

Insurance Measures

All but the simplest insurance measures are beyond the capacity of most MFIs. First, it is difficult to achieve sufficient scale (there needs to be zero chance that all clients will be affected by a disaster at the same time). Second, defining procedures for determining when a payment should be made, for what losses and for how much, are very difficult. Third, cost is usually prohibitive because premiums are proportional to risk. Since poor households generally face greater risk, it is difficult to offer affordable premiums. Therefore, it is usually best if the MFI acts as a link between clients/ groups and reputable insurance companies who can provide general insurance.

Loan Portfolio Management following a Natural Disaster

Accounting of Restructured Loans

The occurrence of a natural disaster can significantly increase the level of risk in the loan portfolio. Some of the financial concessions employed, particularly loan restructuring, might require special accounting treatment to reflect the true level of risk. MFIs need to develop a clear policy regarding how these loans are to be treated in the accounting system. If the MFI considers that there is no additional risk inherent in the restructured loan than was present prior to the disaster event, the loan might be refinanced and recorded in the balance sheet as a "restructured" loan (i.e. as a separate item to "current" loans and "past-due" loans). In doing this, the loan will not contribute to the aging of arrears report and there will be no future loan loss reserve allocated, unless the loan falls into arrears in the future. Alternatively, if the MFI considers that there is increased risk inherent in the restructured loan than was present prior to the disaster, then there might be no change to the way the loan is treated; it will be treated simply as a "past due" loan. Overuse of the refinance option will result in the portfolio appearing healthier than it is in reality. If no refinancing occurs, it will result in the portfolio appearing less healthy than it is. The latter option carries less risk than the former.

Loan Loss Reserves, Write-off Policies, Loan Recovery Policies

Provided restructured loans are treated appropriately, there need not be any alteration to the accounting policy on arrears ageing and delinquent loan write-off. All effort should be taken to ensure that delinquent loans are recovered, either through the client, the loan group, an insurance mechanism, or combination of these.

Availability of Loan Capital

When a significant proportion of the clients of an MFI are severely impacted by a natural disaster, the resulting drain on cash reserves can result in a serious liquidity crisis. MFIs might not be able to offer much needed emergency loans and might need to restrict the withdrawal of savings. Such actions could have a disastrous impact on the credibility of the MFI as a long-term financial intermediary. Therefore, MFIs need to ensure that they have access to sufficient capital, especially when a natural disaster strikes. MFIs should prepare financial models for estimating the amount of additional capital that may be required in the context of a natural disaster, and they should ensure that they have access to sufficient capital, through keeping emergency reserves and/or negotiating a line of credit that can be drawn on at short notice.

CONCLUSION

An MFI that is weak under "normal" conditions will struggle to survive a serious natural disaster. Strong MFIs are better placed to provide relevant and helpful services to their clients. Successful MFIs have effective governance, strong human resource management, accurate and flexible management information systems, and effective portfolio management. They offer services that fit the preferences and needs of poor households, they are efficient, and they operate on a business-like basis. If an MFI wishes to prepare for a disaster event, then its first commitment should be to on-going institutional strengthening. Most MFIs cannot ignore the possibility of being impacted by natural disasters. Many operate in communities and regions where natural disasters are an annual event. It behoves such an MFI to make preparations for the impact of natural disasters on their clients and on the MFI itself. MFIs will be better placed to respond effectively when a disaster strikes if it has worked through the issues, designed policies and products, and negotiated collaboration with DMAs, *before* disaster strikes rather than in the midst of it.

References

Chua, R. T. (1999), Rapid Onset Natural Dısasters-Eight Briefs. Microfinance Best Practices. Development Alternatives. Bethesda.

Brown, W. and Nagarajan, G. (2000), Disaster Loan Funds for Microfinance Institutions. A Look at Emerging Experience. Development Alternatives. Bethesda.

Brown, W. and Nagarajan, G. (2000), Bangladeshi Experience in Adapting Financial Services to Cope with Floods. Implications for the Microfinance Industry. Development Alternatives. Bethesda.

Pantoja, E. (2002), Microfinance and Disaster Risk Management. Experiences and Lessons Learned. Provention Consortium.

Parker, J. and Nagarajan, G. (2000), Can Microfinance Meet the Poor's Financial Needs in Times of Natural Disaster? Development Alternatives. Bethesda.

Nagarajan, G. (1998), Microfinance in the Wake of Natural Disasters. Challenges and Opportunities. Development Alternatives. Bethesda.

Silver, M. (2001), International Best Practices in Disaster Mitigation and Management Recommended for Mongolia. UNDP. Ulaanbaatar. Mongo.

Genetic Analysis of Some Important Quantitative Traits Across Two Environments in Linseed (*Linum Usitatissimum* L.)

SHAILESH P. SOOD*, S. BHATERIA* AND KIRAN PATHANIA*

INTRODUCTION

Oilseeds command second major agricultural crop status in India next to food grains both in terms of production and value (Anon., 2005). Linseed in the world in grown in 30.16 lakh hectares of land with annual production and productivity of 25.69 lakh tones and 852 kg/ha, respectively and in India linseed was grown in 6.4 lakh hectares of land with annual production and productivity of 2.1 lakh tones and 329 kg/ha, respectively (FAO, 2006).Hence, India contributes 21.22 in global linseed area and 8.17 per cent in production. This crop is gaining momentum because of big demand of its grain and fibre for manufacturing several items of industrial significance (Yadav and Srivastva, 2002).

Linseed, being an autogamous crop, genetic improvement has been carried out through conventional breeding methods like selection and hybridization. The variability is pre-requisite for effective selection and it can be generated either through hybridization or mutation breeding or polyploidy. In hybridization, the ability of the parents to combine well depends on the complex interaction among the genes brought in desirable segregants/recombinants which cannot be judged by mere yield performance and adaptation of parents (Hallaur and Mirada, 1981). Combining ability analysis is one important tool for the selection of desirable parents and the reliability of such information increases when drawn over various environments. The present investigation was

* Department of Plant Breeding and Genetics, CSKHPKV, Palampur-176062 (H.P.) INDIA.

therefore undertaken to generate information on the nature and magnitude of gene action and combining ability effects for yield and its component traits and oil content in linseed under varying environments.

MATERIAL AND METHODS

The experimental material, consisting of 56 crosses in a line x tester design involving 14 diverse female parents and 4 well adapted male parents of linseed were laid in a randomized block design replicated two times in two environments (E-I, E-II) comprising two dates of sowing i.e. timely (26th October) and late sown conditions (17th November) during *rabi* 2004-05 at the experimental farm of Department of Plant Breeding and Genetics, CSK Himachal Pradesh Krishi Vishvavidyalaya, Palampur. The parents and F_1s were grown in two rows of 2.5 m length in each replication with row to row and plant to plant spacing of 25 cm and 5 cm, respectively. The recommended package of practices were followed to raise the crop. Analysis of variance was done as per Sukhatme and Amble (1985) and line x tester analysis was done as proposed by Kempthorne (1957).

RESULTS AND DISCUSSION

Analysis of variance for Line x Tester analysis (Table 1) revealed significant differences among parents, females, males and crosses for the characters studied except for secondary branches per plant in parents, females and males. This showed of presence of sufficient genetic variability among the parents, females, males for these characters.

Combining ability analysis pooled over environments revealed sufficient variation for all the traits among lines and testers. The differences between environments were significant for primary and secondary branches per plant, capsules/plant, seed yield per plant and oil content.

The estimates of genetic components of variance together with related genetic parameters for various traits indicated that lines had a higher GCA variance as compared to testers for primary branches per plant, secondary branches per plant, capsules per plant, seeds per capsule, seed yield per plant, harvest index and oil content in both the environments as well as combined over environments. It reveals that environment had significant role in the expression of all the characters. The mean squares due to GCA x environment and SCA x environment interaction were highly significant for all the traits. The average degree of dominance indicated overdominance (>1) for all the characters in both the environments and combined over environments except for seeds per capsule in E-II, where partial dominance (<1) was observed. Narrow sense heritability (h^2ns) estimates are being classified as high (>50 per cent), medium (30-50 per cent) and low (<30 per cent). Days to 50% flowering, days to maturity, plant height and 1000- seed weight showed moderate heritability, whereas primary branches per plant, capsules per plant, seeds per capsule, seed yield per plant, harvest index and oil content showed low heritability.

The contribution of line x tester interaction was more to total variation (35 to 70.35%) in all the traits studied when compared with either lines or testers which clearly indicated that upon crossing sufficient genetic variability can be created for these traits. The share of testers towards total variability was least in comparison to lines and lines x tester interaction. These results are in conformity to the findings of Ratnaparkhi (1998), Kumar *et al.* (2000) and Bhateria *et al.* (2001).

The gca effects reveal that none of the parents had good general combining ability for all the characters studied. Significant General combining ability effects, significant values were observed in nine female parents *viz.*, KL-223, Chambal, Nagarkot, Binwa, LCK-9816, Parvati, Himalini, KL-168 and KL-187 and two male parents, Surbhi and Kangra local for as many as four to nine traits on the strength of the magnitude of GCA effects for various traits over environments.

The preponderance of non-additive gene action (for days to 50 per cent flowering, days to maturity, plant height, primary branches/plant, secondary branches/plant, capsules/plant, seeds/capsule, 1000-seed weight, seed yield/plant, harvest index and oil content, is in accordance with the earlier studies of Thakur and Bhateria (1991), Tak (1996), Patel *et al.* (1997), Mahto and Rahman (1998), Kumar *et al.* (2000) and Bhateria *et al.* (2001). However, Yadav and Srivastava (2002), found highly significant SCA and GCA for early growth vigour, days to 50 per cent flowering, days to maturity, 1000-seed weight and seed yield/plant indicating importance of both non-additive and additive gene actions. Out of fourteen maternal parents, four (LCK-9816, Parvati, Himalini, KL-168) were good general combiner for seed yield and related traits as well as for oil content. Among male parents, two (Surbhi and KL-224) were found poor general combiners for seed yield, but were good general combiners for yield related traits and oil content and one male parent KL-221 was good general combiner for seed yield and its component traits but was poor general combiner for oil content. It is therefore, suggested that intermating of randomly selected progenies in early segregating generations (especially in F_2 and F_3) obtained by crossing these parents will release the hidden genetic variability through breakage of undesirable linkages involved in different characters. Thus generating an elite population for selection of high yielding lines in advanced generations.

Low heritability in case of primary branches per plant, capsules per plant, seeds per capsule, seed yield per plant, harvest index and oil content suggests non-fixable component of variation governing these traits. On the other hand moderate heritability in case of days to flowering, days to maturity, plant height and 1000- seed weight implying that these traits can be improved by making selections among the recombinants obtained through segregating populations. Since gene action involved in crosses was of non- additive type with low and medium heritability, therefore, direct selection for such traits will not be effective. Hence, these crosses can be exploited in subsequent generations for isolating desirable segregants.

References

Anonymous (2005), Low Cost Production Technology for Oilseed Crops. Directorate of Oilseeds Research Rajendranagar, Hyderabad (A.P.).

Bhateria, S., A. Pathania, J. K. Sharma, D. Badiyala & J. C. Bhandari (2001), Combining Ability for Seed Yield and its Components in Linseed (*Linum usitatissimum* L.). *Journal of Oilseeds Research*, 18, 44-47.

FAO (2006), Production Year Book. Food and Agricultural Organization, Rome 56, 127.

Hallaur, A. R. & J. P. Mirada (1981), Quantitative Genetics in Maize Breeding. Iowa State University Press Ames.

Kempthorne, O. (1957), An Introduction to Genetic Statistics. John Wiley and Sons, New York, p. 458.

Kumar, M., P.K. Singh & N. P. Singh (2000), Line x Tester Analysis for Seed Yield and its Components in Linseed (*Linum usitatissimum* L.). *Annals of Agricultural Research*, 21, 485-489.

Mahto, C. & M. H. Rahman (1998), Line x Tester Analysis of Seed Yield and its Components in Linseed (*Linum usitatissimum* L.). *Journal of Oilseeds Research*, 15, 242-246.

Patel, J. A., Y. K. Gupta, S. B. Patel and J. N. Patel (1997), Combining Ability Analysis Over Environments in Linseed. *Madras Agricultural Journal*, 84: 188-191.

Ratnaparkhi, R. D., N. N. Kolte & P. W. Khorgade (1998), Line x Tester Analysis for Combining Ability in Linseed (*Linum usitatissimum* L.). *PKV Research Journal* 22, 3-6.

Sukhatme, P.V. and V. N. Amble (1985), Statistical Methods for Agricultural Workers, ICAR, New Delhi.

Tak, G. M. (1996), Gene Action in Linseed. *Advances in Plant Sciences* 9, 99-102.

Thakur, H. L. and S. Bhateria (1991), Line x Tester Analysis for Combining Ability in Linseed. *Journal of Oilseeds Research*, 8, 14-19.

Yadav, R. K. and S. B. L. Srivastava (2002), Combining Ability Analysis Over Environments in Linseed (*Linum usitatissimum* L.). *Crop Research*, 23, 277-282.

Application of Integer Programming Model for Optimizing Design Facility Using Lean Manufacturing (A Case Study)

B. VIJAYA RAMNATH[*#], C. ELANCHEZHIAN[*] AND R. KESAVAN[***]

INTRODUCTION

The globalization and strong competition in current market places have forced companies to change their ways of doing business. Roberto Panizzolo describes the challenges posed by lean production principles for operation management. He developed a model which accurately define and operationalize the lean production concept characterizing different areas of the company like product design, process and equipment, manufacturing planning and control and customer, supplier relationship.

Ben Naylor, Mohamed M. Nair and Danny Berry concluded that as lean thinking and agile manufacturing paradigms here had been developed there has been a tendency to view them in a progression and in isolation. They dealt a case study which demonstrates how agility and leanness have been combined successfully within one supply chain to meet customer requirement.

Ram Narasimhan, Morgan suink and Soo Wook Kim made an attempt to determine whether lean and agile forms occur with any degree of regularity in manufacturing plant. They found that while the pursuit of agility might presume leanness, pursuit of leanness might not presume agility.

* Research Scholar, Department of Production Technology, M.I.T. Campus, Anna University, Chrompet, Chennai-600 044, Tamilnadu, India, (*Corresponding Author : E-mail: vijayaramnathb@gmail.com, bvijayaramnath@yahoo.com*).

** Asst. Professor, Department of Production Technology, M.I.T. Campus, Anna University, Chrompet, Chennai- Chennai-600 044, Tamilnadu, India.

This paper aims at designing the sprockets using plastic. The material chosen is Ultra High Molecular Weight High Density Polyethylene (UHMHDPE).

The following are the steps involved in replacing the metal cycle sprocket with plastic:

1. Designing the sprocket using Pro/E.
2. Analysing the sprocket using ANSYS
3. Preparing the mold using pro mold.
4. Injection molding of plastic sprocket

At the end of Ansys analysis, it was found that the design is safe. This can be validated from the fact that the calculated working shear stress value is less than the yield stress value. The results obtained from ANSYS also stands as a proof for this.

PROBLEM IDENTIFICATION

Problem with Conventional Design Process

The conventional design process consumes more time for design .Here, validation is done by real time fabrication of sprocket which consumes time and cost. After fabrication, the sprocket checked for its strength. If it fails again redesign of the product is done which is followed by real time fabrication. The above said procedure is repeated till the product valid for its strength and safety.

MASTHEMATICAL MODELLING OF COST DESIGN PROCESS

Conventional Design Process

In the present method of manufacturing, initially the modeling is done for the sprocket. The core and cavity is designed in the next stage. Now, by using above designed core and cavity, the sprocket is produced by compression molding process. Then it is checked for its strength and safety. Here, it took three trials for producing correct model. The cost and time of modeling and manufacturing is given below,

Let,

T_m = Time for modeling (in hrs)

T_C = Time for designing core and cavity (in hrs)

C_D = Cost for die making (in Rs)

C_C = Cost of compression molding (in Rs.)

C_m = Cost for modeling (in Rs.)

C_{DC} = Cost of designing core and cavity (in Rs.)

∴ Total cost for producing a sprocket = $(T_m \times C_m) + (T_C \times C_{DC}) + C_D + C_C$

Here,

C_m = Rs. 2000 per hour

C_{DC} = Rs. 3000 per hour.

C_D = Rs. 45000/-

C_C = Rs. 8000/-

∴ Total cost for producing a sprocket - Trail I

= $(T_m \times C_m) + (T_C \times C_{DC}) + C_D + C_C$

= (8 ×2000) + (15 ×3000) + 45000 + 8000

= Rs. 1,14,000

∴ Total cost for producing a sprocket - Trial II

= $(T_m \times C_m) + (T_C \times C_{DC}) + C_D + C_C$

= (5 × 2000) + (8 × 3000) + 45000 + 8000

= Rs. 87,000

While analyzing the sprocket produced for its permissible value, it is not giving safety result. Cracks are formed at the base of the sprocket. So, ribs are introduced in the model and again modeling, core and cavity design and compression molding is done.

The total cost and time incurred for trail III given below:

∴ Total cost for producing a sprocket - Trail III

= $(T_m \times C_m) + (T_C \times C_{DC}) + C_D + C_C$

= (3 × 2000) + (6 × 3000) + 45000 + 8000

= Rs. 77,000

While analyzing the sprocket for its permissible value, it shows the result are within the safety limit. So, we can use the model created in this trial III as reference design and entire production shall be started as long term process.

Therefore, the total cost involved to produce a standard reference design in conventional design is as follows:

Total cost for producing standard reference design

= (Total cost for Trial I) +
(Total cost for Trial II) +
(Total cost for Trial III)

= 1,14,000 + 87,000 + 77,000

= Rs. 2,78,000

PROPOSED METHODOLOGY: LEAN MANUFACTURING

International motor vehicle programme defines lean manufacturing is lean, because it consumes less of everything. Lean is a set of tools which leads for achieving following goals like reduced cycle time, reduced inventory levels, increased productivity and output and reducing defects and wastages.

Lean Enterprises Research Centre (LERC) broken down manufacturing company activities like:

(i) Value-added activity - 5%

(ii) Non-value added activity - 60%

(iii) Necessary non-value added activity - 35%

All manufacturers are mainly aims to reduce the 60% non value added activities in their plant, which are in the form of wastes.

Major Kinds of Wastes

There are 7 main types of wastes identified as a part of lean production system as follows:

Over Production

It is producing more than the customer demands.

Defects

It is physical defects added with the product during manufacturing.

Inventory

It is maintaining high level of raw material.

Transportation

It is any movement that does not add value to the product.

Waiting

It is idle time for workers or machines. (More time consuming for loading and unloading of the component.)

Motion

It is any unnecessary physical motion or difficult physical movements due to poorly designed ergonomics, which slow down the worker and give fatigue to them.

Over-Processing

It is doing more processing work than the customer requirement.

One of major waste identified in conventional design is product "Correction time" which leads for more lead time for the product release. This paper mainly aims to reduce this correction time with lean manufacturing principles. Here, the new plastic sprocket is designed using ProE-promold software for modeling. The modeled sprocket was analysed for its maximum stress withstanding capacity using ANSYS analysis software. The above mentioned ProE and ANSYS software discussed briefly in the following sessions.

Lean Based Design

The lean concept of design aims to reduce design time, correction time, cost for designing the standard reference mold model. In this model, after creating the model in Pro-E, it is analysed for its permissible values by using ANSYS package. By doing so, if any error occurs in the design of sprocket, it is redesigned and analysed immediately without real time fabrication as in conventional design process.

About Using Pro/mold Design

Pro/Mold Design is an optional module in Pro/Engineer that provides the tool to simulate the mold design process within Pro/Engineer. This module lets you create, modify, and analyse the sprocket, mold components and assemblies, and quickly update them to the changes in the design model. The sprocket is molded using this Pro-mold design module.

Validation of Lean Based Design

In this Lean based design, using ProE sprocket is modeled and is exported to ANSYS for carrying out analysis. The cost and time involved for both modeling and analysis is given in the following table. It took six trials to completely design a valid and safe sprocket.

Table 1
Time For Modeling and Analysing

Trial	*Machine A Time for modeling (α) hrs*	*Machine B Time for analyzing (β) hrs*	*Total cost (γ) Rs.*
1	8	4	24,000
2	6	4	18,500
3	5	3	16,500
4	5	4	18,000
5	2	3	10,500
6	2	2	9,000

To find optimal time for modeling and analysis, a relationship is prepared between α, β, and γ as given by the following equations,

$$\gamma = A\alpha^2 + B\alpha\beta + C\beta^2 + D\alpha + E\beta + F \quad (1)$$

$$64A + 32B + 16C + 8D + 4E + F = 24{,}000 \quad (2)$$

$$36A + 24B + 16C + 6D + 4E + F = 18{,}500 \quad (3)$$

$$25A + 15B + 9C + 5D + 3E + F = 16{,}500 \quad (4)$$

$$25A + 20B + 16C + 5D + 4E + F = 18{,}000 \quad (5)$$

$$4A + 6B + 9C + 2D + 3E + F = 10{,}500 \quad (6)$$

$$4A + 4B + 4C + 2D + 2E + F = 9{,}000 \quad (7)$$

while solving above equations, we obtained

A = 750

B = -4500

C = 6750

D = 10250

E = -23250

F = 23000

Now substitute the above values in (1), we get,

$$750\alpha^2 - 4500\alpha\beta + 6750\beta^2 + 10250\alpha - 23250\beta + 23000 = \gamma \quad (8)$$

differentiate (8) with respect to α and β; we obtained,

$$\frac{\partial \gamma}{\partial \alpha} = 1500\alpha - 4500\beta + 10250 \quad (9)$$

$$\frac{\partial \gamma}{\partial \beta} = -4500\alpha + 13500\beta - 23250 \quad (10)$$

Now find second order derivative of (9) and (10);

$$\frac{\partial^2 \gamma}{\partial \alpha^2} = 1500 \quad (11)$$

$$\frac{\partial^2 \gamma}{\partial \beta^2} = 13500 \quad (12)$$

Since the values of second order derivatives are positive, this is minimization problem, while solving (9) and (10) we obtained,

α = 5.15 hrs

β = 3.9 hrs

which are the optimal value of modeling and analysis time using lean based design. While substituting above obtained a and b value in (8), we get γ = Rs. 17,979 which is optimal cost of design for each trial. This shows the lean based design is optimal while compared to the conventional design process.

The Research and Development (R & D) department received two types of design of sprocket from their customer (X and Y). To make the optimal design of above two sprocket the Research and Development department decides to design two types of Sprocket using Computer A (for Modelling) and Computer B (for Analysing). Sprocket X requires two hours on Computer A and six hours on Computer B. Sprocket Y requires Five hours on Computer A and five hours on Computer B. There are 16 hours of time per day available on Computer A and 30 hours on Computer B. Sprocket X and Y varies only with small change in diameter.

The profit gained by designing both the dolls is same. They want to know what should be the daily design of each of the two sprockets. To solve this situation integer linear programming model is selected to find optimum number of design that can be done for sprockets X and Y.

Let the Research and Development department decide to design x_1 number of sprocket X and x_2 number of sprocket Y so as to maximize the profit. Now the complete formulation of the Linear Programming Problem is given by,

$$\text{Maximize } Z = x_1 + x_2$$

Subject to

$$2x_1 + 5x_2 \leq 16$$

$$6x_1 + 5x_2 \geq 30$$

and $x_1, x_2 \geq 0$ are integers,

Ignoring the integrality condition and introducing the non-negative slack variables x_3 and x_4, the standard form of the continuous LPP becomes,

$$\text{Maximise } Z = x_1 + x_2 + 0s_1 + 0s_2$$

subject to,

$$2x_1 + 5x_2 + 0s_1 + 0s_2 = 16$$

$$6x_1 + 5x_2 + 0s_1 + 0s_2 = 30$$

and $\quad x_1, x_2, s_1, s_2 \geq 0$

The initial basic feasible solution is given by: $s_1 = 16$, $s_2 = 30$ (basic), $x_1 = x_2 = 0$ (non basic).

Initial Iteration

C_j	1	1	0	0				
X_j	x_1	x_2	s_1	s_2	X_B	Y_B	C_B	Ratio
	2	5	1	0	16	s_1	0	8
	(6)	5	0	1	30	s_2	0	5*
Z_j	0	0	0	0	0			
$Z_j - C_j$	-1	-1	0	0				

Since the condition $Z_j - C_j \geq 0$ is not satisfied, the solution is not optimum. It has to be improved by introducing x_1 and dropping s_2.

First Iteration

C_j	1	1	0	0				
X_j	x_1	x_2	s_1	s_2	X_B	Y_B	C_B	Ratio
	0	(10/3)	1	-1/3	6	s_1	0	18/10 = 9/5
	1	5/6	0	1/6	5	x_1	1	30/5 = 6
Z_j	1	5/6	0	1/6	5			
$Z_j - C_j$	0	-1/6	0	1/6				

Since the condition $Z_j - C_j \geq 0$ is not satisfied, the solution is not optimum. It is to be improved by introducing x_2 and dropping s_1.

Second Iteration

C_j	1	1	0	0				
X_j	x_1	x_2	s_1	s_2	X_B	Y_B	C_B	Ratio
	0	1	3/10	-1/10	9/5	x_2	1	
	1	0	-1/4	1/4	7/2	x_1	1	
Z_j	1	1	1/20	3/20	53/10			
$Z_j - C_j$	0	0	1/20	3/20				

Since all $Z_j - C_j \geq 0$, the current basic feasible solution is optimal and a non-integer.

i.e., Maximise $Z = \frac{53}{10}$, $x_1 = \frac{7}{2}$, $x_2 = \frac{9}{5}$.

In order to obtain the optimum integer solution, we have to construct a fractional cut constraint.

Now, $x_1 = \frac{7}{2} = 3 + \frac{1}{2} = [X_{B1}] + f_1$; $x_2 = \frac{9}{5} = 1 + \frac{4}{5} = [X_{B2}] + f_2$

Therefore Maximise $\{f_1, f_2\}$ = Maximise $\left\{\frac{1}{2}, \frac{4}{5}\right\} = \frac{4}{5}$, which corresponds to the first row (called the source row).

Then, from this source row we have: $1 + \frac{4}{5} = x_1 + x_2 + \frac{3}{10} s_1 - \frac{1}{10} s_2$

Expressing the negative fraction as a sum of a negative integer and a non-negative fraction, we have,

$$1 + \frac{4}{5} = x_2 + \frac{3}{10} s_1 + \left(-1 + \frac{9}{10}\right) s_2$$

Therefore, the fractional cut (Gomorian) construct is given by:

$$\frac{3}{10} s_1 + \frac{9}{10} s_2 \geq \frac{4}{5}$$

$$\Rightarrow \quad \frac{-3}{10} s_1 - \frac{9}{10} s_2 \leq -\frac{4}{5}$$

$$\Rightarrow \quad \frac{-3}{10} s_1 - \frac{9}{10} s_2 + Gs_1 = -\frac{4}{5}$$

Where, Gs_1 is the Gomorian slack.

Adding this fractional cut constraint at the bottom of the above optimum simplex table, we have :

C_j	1	1	0	0				
X_j	x_1	x_2	s_1	s_2	Gs1	X_B	Y_B	C_B
	0	1	3/10	-1/10	0	9/5	x_2	1
	1	0	-1/4	1/4	0	7/2	X_1	1
	0	0	(-3/10)	-9/10	1	-4/5	Gs_1	0
Z_j						53/10		
$Z_j - C_j$	0	0	1/20	3/20	0			

Here the solution is optimal but infeasible.

To find a feasible optimal solution, we have to use the dual simplex method. Since $Gs_1 = \frac{4}{5}$, Gs_1 leaves the basis. To find the entering variable: Also, Maximise $\left\{\frac{Z_j - C_j}{a_{ik}}, a_{ik} < 0\right\}$ Maximise $= \left\{\frac{\frac{1}{20}}{\frac{-3}{10}}, \frac{\frac{3}{20}}{\frac{-9}{10}}\right\} =$ Maximise $\left\{\frac{-1}{6}, \frac{-1}{6}\right\} = \frac{-1}{6}$, which corresponds to x_3 and x_4. We shall choose s_1 arbitrarily as the entering variable.

Third Iteration

C_j	1	1	0	0				
X_j	x_1	x_2	s_1	s_2	Gs1	X_B	Y_B	C_B
	0	1	0	-1	1	1	x_2	1
	1	0	0	1	-5/6	25/6	X_1	1
	0	0	1	3	-10/3	8/3	s_1	0
Z_j						31/6		
Z_j - C_j	0	0	0	0	1/6			

Since all $Z_j - C_j \geq 0$ and all $X_{Bi} \geq 0$. the current solution is feasible and optimal but a non-integer. To obtain the optimum integer solution, we have to construct a fractional cut constraint.

Now,
$$x_1 = \frac{25}{6} = 4 + \frac{1}{6} = [X_{B1}] + f_1$$

$$s_1 = \frac{8}{3} = 2 + \frac{2}{3} = [X_{B2}] + f_2$$

Therefore Maximise $[f_1, f_3]$ = Maximise $\left[\frac{1}{6}, \frac{2}{3}\right] = \frac{2}{3}$, which corresponds to the third row.

From this source row, we have: $2 + \frac{2}{3} = s_1 + 3s_2 - \frac{10}{3} Gs_1 = s_1 + 3s_2 + \left(-4 + \frac{2}{3}\right) Gs_1$

Therefore, the fractional cut (Gomorian) construct is given by: $\frac{2}{3}Gs_1 \geq \frac{2}{3} \Rightarrow \frac{-2}{3} Gs_1 \leq \frac{-2}{3} \Rightarrow Gs_1 + Gs_2 = \frac{-2}{3}$ Where Gs_2 is the Gomorian slack.

Adding this fractional cut constraint at the bottom of the above optimum simplex table and using the dual simplex method, we have:

C_j	1	1	0	0	0	0				
X_j	x_1	x_2	s_1	s_2	Gs_1	Gs_2	X_B	Y_B	C_B	Ratio
0	1	0	-1	1	0	1	x_2	1		
1	0	0	1	-5/6	0	25/6	x_1	1		
0	0	1	3	-10/3	0	8/3	x_3	0		
0	0	0	0	(-2/3)	1	-2/3	Gs_2	0		
Z_j	1	1	0	0	1/6	0	31/6			
$Z_j - C_j$	0	0	0	3	1/6	0				

Since $Gs_2 = \frac{-2}{3}$, Gs_2 leaves the basis. Now, Maximise

$$\left\{\frac{Z_j - C_j}{a_{jk}},\ a_{jk} < 0\right\} = \left\{\frac{\frac{1}{6}}{\frac{-2}{3}}\right\} = \frac{-1}{4}$$ which corresponds to Gs_1 So, Gs_1 enters the basis.

Fourth Iteration

C_j	1	1	0	0	0	0				
X_j	x_1	x_2	s_1	s_2	Gs_1	Gs_2	X_B	Y_B	C_B	Ratio
	0	1	0	-1	0	3/2	0	x_2	1	
	1	0	0	1	0	-5/4	5	x_1	1	
	0	0	1	3	0	-5	6	s_1	0	
	0	0	0	0	1	-3/2	1	Gs_1	0	
Z_j	1	1	0	0	0	0	5			
$Z_j - C_j$	0	0	0	0	0	¼				

Since all $(Z_j - C_j) \geq 0$ and all $X_{Bi} \geq 0$, and are integers, the current solution is feasible and integer optimal.

Therefore, the optimal solution to the new problem is:

$$\text{Maximise } Z = 5,\ x_1 = 5,\ x_2 = 0.$$

That is the Research and Development Department should design five numbers of sprockets X alone in order to get a maximum profit by utilizing the available computers.

Design Validation

The stress obtained by analyzing the modeled plastic sprocket using ANSYS package is 25.87 N/mm^2. The permissible shear stress for plastic is 27.86 N/mm^2. While comparing the stress values obtained through ANSYS evaluation and permissible stress value, all are less than permissible value which shows the design is safe and valid.

CONCLUSION

In this paper a plastic cycle sprocket was designed using UHMHDPE with lean principles. A comparison is made between conventional design and lean based design. As the conventional design process consumes more time, Lean based design is done for reducing cycle time and floor space. The result shows that Lean based design consumes less lead time and lesser cost as compared to the conventional one. Also, a mathematical analysis was carried out to find optimal cost for designing the sprocket through lean based design. The analysis shows the design was optimal and feasible as compared to the conventional system of design. Also the sprocket designed is safe and valid as its stress value is lesser than permissible stress value of plastic. The optimization study shows that sprocket type X can be designed five times per day to have maximum profit.

References

E. Mohebbi (2007), "A Note on Production Control Model for Facility with Limited Storage Capacity in a Random Environment ", *European Journal of Operational Research,* June, pp. 562-570.

Rachna Shan, Peter T. Ward (2007), "*Designing and Developing Measures of Lean Production*", *Journal of Operation Management,* pp. 1-21.

Ram Narasimhan, Morgan Swink, Soo Wook Kim (2006), "Disentangling Leanness and Agility: An Empirical Investigation", *Journal of Operation Management,* 24, pp. 440-457.

S. Grewal, K. Sarren (2006), "Development of Model for Lean Improvement: A Case Study", *Industrial Engineering Journal,* 5, pp. 24-27.

Durk-Jouke, Jannes Slomp (2005), "*Simulation and Gaming as a Support Tool for Lean Manufacturing System*", in Winter Simulation Conference Proceedings.

"*Introduction to Lean Manufacturing*", Mekong Capital, June 2004, pp. 2-9.

V. Crute, Y. Ward, S. Brown, and A. Graves (2003), "*Implementing Lean in Aerospace- Challanging the Assumptions and Understanding the Challenges,*" Technovation, pp. 917-928.

Nick Oliver, Rick Delbridge, Harry Barton (2002), *"Lean Production and Manufacturing Performance Improvement in Japan, The UK and US 1994-2001"*, ESRC Business Research, University of Cambridge.

LUIS M. Sanchez, Rakesh Nagi (2001), "A Review of Agile Manufacturing System", *International Journal of Production Research*, 39(16), pp. 3651-3600.

Y. Monden (1998), *"Toyota Production System"*, Springer - 3rd edition.

C. Spaccatotella (1998), *"Lean Manufacturing Design Through Simulation Analysis"*, SAE Transaction, No 982119.

S. Shingo, *"Quick Change Over for Operators"*, The SMED System, Productivity Press, Portland, 1996.

E. G. Hoffman (1996), *"Setup Reduction Through Effective Work Holding"*, Industrial Press, New York.

J. Claunch (1996), *"Setup Time reduction,"* Irwin.

J. Womack, D. T. Jones, *"Lean Thinking - Banish Waste and Create Wealth in Your Corporation"*, Simor and Schuster, New York.

J. Womack, D.T. Jones, and D. Ross (1990), *"The Machine that Changed the World"*, Maxwell Macmillan International, New York.

Roberto Panizzolo (1998), "Applying the Lessons Learned from 27 Lean Manufacturers, The Relevance of Relationship Management", *Int. Journal of Production Economics*, 55, pp. 223-240.

Ben Naylor, Mohamed M.Nair, Denny Berry (1999), "Legility: Integrating the Lean and Agile Manufacturing Paradigms in the Total Supply Chain", *Int. Journal of Production Economics*, , 62, pp. 107-118.

Human Right Violations in India: A View

S. VIJAYEN*

INTRODUCTION

The Government of India have set up a forum for redressal of human rights violations by constituting the National Human Rights Commission (NHRC) and provided for the setting up of State Human Rights Commission (SHRC) under the Protection of Human Rights Act, 1993. The Constitution of India has provisions and guarantees for safeguarding almost the entire gamut of civil and political rights. Directive Principles of State Policy further require the States to ensure the promotion and protection of social, cultural and economic rights, particularly of the weaker sections of the society, so as to bring about a just and equitable social order, leading to an overall improvement in the quality of life for all sections of the society. The civil and criminal laws of our country have also in-built mechanism to safeguard the rights of the individuals and provide special protection to the most vulnerable sections of the society.

Human Rights Education and Training

A National Action Plan for Human Rights Education, adopted by the Government of India, envisages promotion and awareness of human rights to all sections of the society. Specific target groups have been identified such as schools, colleges and universities. Government officials, armed forces, prison officials and law officers are also sensitised to the protection of human rights. The Ministry of Home Affairs has taken various initiatives for the spread of human rights education; such as Human Rights courses have been introduced as a

* Lecturer (SS), Economics Wing, Directorate of Distance Education, Annamalai University, Annamalainagar.

part of the training for the Border Security Force and the Central Reserve Police Force. Human Rights courses have also been introduced as a part of the training at the National Police Academy and Police Training Colleges.

Transparency and Commitment to Human Rights

The Government have cooperated fully with various human rights agencies functioning under United Nations (UN) and have been responding in an appropriate manner to specific complaints of alleged human rights violations. The Government have also, in their obligation under International Convention, been sending information and replies to specific issues and questions received from various Rapporteurs of the UN High Commission for Human Rights including complaints of human rights violations received from Permanent Mission of India, Geneva through the Ministry of External Affairs.

Memorandum of Understanding (MoU) with ICRC

In consonance with their policy of transparency, the Government of India have signed an MoU with the International Committee of the Red Cross (ICRC) in June, 1995, which provides the Delegates of the ICRC access to detention centres where individuals, arrested or detained in connection with the situation prevailing in J&K, are lodged. Since the operation of the MoU in 1995, the ICRC delegates have made 832 visits and have visited/revisited 67 places of detention and registered 10,388 detainees up to December, 2007. The NHRC was set up under the Protection of Human Rights Act, 1993. It is headed by a former Chief Justice of the Supreme Court. One of the primary functions of NHRC is to receive complaints and initiate investigations into violations of Human Rights by public servants by acts of commission and omission through negligence on their part to prevent violation of human rights when brought to its notice within one year of the commission of such violation. During the year 2007-08 (up to December 31, 2007), 76,444 cases were registered by the Commission for consideration. The Commission disposed off 73,618 cases, which includes cases brought forward from the previous years, during the period up to December 31, 2007, including recommendation for payment of interim relief in 86 cases amounting to Rs.148.94 lakh. The Commission has set up a Training Division with a focus on imparting training to various stakeholders. The emphasis, wherever possible, is on collaboration with renowned training institutions so that these programmes become self-sustaining.

Custodial Violence

Custodial violence has been one of the core concerns of the NHRC and with each succeeding year the Commission has deepened and widened its analysis and directives in regard to such matters. On their part, in accordance with guidelines, the agencies of the States/UTs have been found prompt in informing the Commission within 24 hours about occurrence of incidents of custodial death. During the period April 1, 2007 to December 31, 2007, a total of 1,459 cases of custodial deaths (1,315 cases of judicial custodial deaths and 144 cases of police custody deaths) were reported to the Commission by the State Governments/ UT Administrations. The cases of custodial deaths are reviewed in the Commission, with the help of its Investigation Division, and appropriate orders passed in respect of them. During the period, the Commission recommended payment of interim relief of Rs.81.45 lakh to the nextof-kin of the victims in 51 cases of custodial deaths.

Trafficking in Women and Children

The Commission completed an Action Research on Trafficking in Women and Children in India in collaboration with the United Nations Development Fund for Women (UNIFEM) and the Institute of Social Sciences, New Delhi, in order to know the trends, dimensions, factors and responses related to trafficking in women and children. Besides requesting all the concerned agencies to implement the recommendations made in the report, the Commission itself has prepared a comprehensive Plan of Action to implement them in true spirit. The Plan of Action has been disseminated among all stakeholders.

Human Rights Awareness, Education and Training

The Commission attaches considerable significance to the dissemination of information and awareness on human rights issues. It has already come out with several publications, both priced and non-priced, on variety of subjects related to human rights. The Commission which had in December, 2004 released a collection of eight booklets under the "Know Your Rights" series, continued its endeavor to have it translated in all the regional languages. The booklet series is now available in 8 regional languages apart from English and Hindi. The process of its publication in 5 other regional languages is underway. As a part of its objective of human rights education at the University level, the Commission continued to hold Summer Internship programme, which was conducted from May 15, 2007 to June 14, 2007.

The Winter Internship Programme commenced on December 17, 2007 and concluded on January 16, 2008 and 46 Interns attended the programme. During these internship programmes, the selected students were sensitised towards the activities of the Commission and human rights values.

CASTE SYSTEM IN INDIA

India is a country with a lot of traditions, culture, and beauty. The most pathetic part of these traditions is an unwanted, ugly, and inhuman structure called the *Caste System*. One cannot but feel ashamed of the caste system as this system continue to discriminate the human persons and stratifies them into different groups. In Hindu society, caste is still the most powerful factor in determining a person's dignity. Socially, Dalits are placed outside the four-fold graded caste system of Indian Society. Hindu Scriptures divide the people on the basis of birth (descent-based discrimination). The social structure of India is stratified, with inbuilt inequalities and injustices, based on the caste system sanctified by *Brahmins (Hindus)*. Although social stratification exists in almost all societies, the caste system is quite unique to Indian society. Sanctioned by the religious philosophical system, the Dalits are socially placed outside the four-fold caste system and they are referred to as the fifth caste (outcaste).

India's caste system has existed for more than 3000 years and appears to be deliberately and intentionally developed by the Brahmins (priests) in order to maintain their superiority over the other castes. Typically, the caste system is divided into 4 distinct classes. This is referred as "Varnas". At the top the caste hierarchies are the Brahmins, the priestly class. According to the Hindu religious book called *Manusmruti*, the Brahmins came from the head of God. They are eligible for learning, teaching and perform religious ceremonies. The others cannot teach and perform sacrifice, hence they have 100% control on religion, education and Vedas. Next come the Kshatriyas. The people in this class are warrior, and according to *Manusmruti*, they originated from the shoulder of God. They are eligible for learning. Their work is to protect the people by waging war against the enemies. The Vaisyas are the trading class and came from the thigh of God. Their work is to trade and feed the above two classes. Finally stand the Sudras. This is the servants class and came from the feet of God. Their work is to do all menial work for the above three classes. They are not entitled to learn anything. In addition to the above four classes, there is a fifth class called "untouchables" or outcaste. They literally have no caste and means oppressed, downtrodden, broken and exploited social group. Such a rigid caste system is not found anywhere in the world outside India. Once born in the caste, a person's status is predetermined and immutable. Birth decides any talent the person may develop, and one cannot alter one's status or wealth the person may accumulate. Similarly, the caste in which a person is born predetermines what profession or activities he will pursue. What is surprising is that even today most Hindus who are living abroad still practice the caste system in their country of residence.

HUMAN RIGHTS VIOLATIONS AGAINST DALITS IN INDIA

According to the Hindu religious belief, "All human beings are not born equal." This creates caste-based discrimination against Dalits, which is then open to various forms of violence against them, which include public humiliation, torture, rape, beating, and killing, etcetera. The untouchability is the basis for atrocities and violence, denial of basic needs, land rights, legal discrimination, infringement of civil liberties, inferior or no people status, de-humanizing living and working conditions, impoverishment, mal-nourishment, bad health conditions, high levels of illiteracy and continuing social ostracism is continue to the reason for human rights violations against dalits. Even today, in rural India, Dalits are prevented from most common social activities such as sharing water, food and drinks. They are barred from wearing shoes when meeting high caste Hindus. They are not allowed to cycle through village streets in which higher caste people live. They can be publicly dehumanized by small crimes such as shooing away a chicken, dogs, and other pets that belong to higher caste people. They are discriminated against, denied access to land, forced to work in the most degrading conditions, and are routinely abused by the hands of the police and higher caste Hindus who enjoy government protection. Most Dalits continue to live in precarious conditions and are not allowed to use the same well, visit the temples, drink from the same cups in tea stalls or even cannot claim the land that legally belongs to them. Most Dalits continue to live in extreme poverty, without land, and they lack opportunities for better employment and education.

According to the National Commission of Human rights of India, more than 62,000 human rights violations are recorded annually. On average, two Dalits are assaulted every hour, three Dalit women and children are raped, two Dalits are murdered, and at least two Dalits are tortured or burned every day. Due to space, it is not possible to describe an individual human rights abuse. Following are some of the most inhuman "Human Right Violations" that took place in recent time in India. For instance, recently, five Dalits in the Northern district of India, Haryana, were lynched by a mob of 4,000 Hindus on the allegation that they skinned the cow (according to Hinduism, the cow is considered holy), as these victims denied a bribe to police. In another incident, a four-month pregnant Dalit women from Tamilnadu district (Southern part of India), was beaten by upper caste Hindus from the same village. She was stripped naked and paraded in front of the village as well as her family members. Later, police beat her in jail, which resulted in her miscarriage.

Less than 3.5% culprits are prosecuted for such crimes, and out of 10 cases of atrocities against Dalits, only one is prosecuted. The problem is not the law; implementation is a total failure because the less than 15% high caste Hindus who control 85% of the wealth, power, justice system, police and 100% of the media. Hence, the culprits go unpunished. Most importantly, these violations are not only performed against Dalits, but also on other minority communities in India. For the last few years, Hindu masses have been directly associated with the human rights violations against Muslims, Christians and Sikhs throughout India. For instance, Hindus killed more than 3,000 Muslims in a Mosque demolition in 1992. In 1994, more than 4,000 Sikhs in the Delhi area were killed in Communal riots. In recent years, more than 2,000 Muslims in Gujrat and hundreds of Christians have been killed.

Human Right Violations against Dalit Children

According to the national Commission for Scheduled Caste (SC) and Scheduled Tribes (ST), there are an estimated 115 million children working in slavery, and amongst those, approximately 80-90% are Dalits who work as bonded labour in order to pay off debt. In slavery, children, often from poor families, are picked by a high caste restaurant or shop owner and are forced to work 16-18 hours a day at wages of not more than 2-3 dollars per year. Their denial to the order of their owner or trying to escape can result in severe beating and no food and water for several days. According to government statistics, an estimated 800,000 Dalits are manual scavengers who are involve in clearing human feces from pubic and private latrines and disposing of dead animals. A recent survey conducted by two teams of National Geographic stated that "in one toilet there can be more than 400 seats which all have to be manually cleaned. This is the lowest occupation in the world, which is performed by the community occupying the lowest status in the caste system". In addition to the above, there are approximately 50,000 Dalits girls who are forced to practice a Hindu religious practice of child prostitution, called *Devdasi*. Devadasis, literally meaning "female servant of god," and they usually belong to the Dalit community. Amazingly, this practice still exists in Indian states like Andhra Pradesh, Karnatka, Orissa and Maharashtra. Once dedicated, the girl is unable to marry, is forced to become a prostitute for upper-caste community members, and is eventually auctioned off to an urban brothel, where she may die due of many sexual diseases, including HIV/AIDS.

Human Rights Violations against Dalit Women

According to Arpita Anant, researcher on the behalf of South Asia Partnership of Canada, Dalit women in India face the triple burden: caste, class and gender. As stated by another woman activist in India, "No one practices un-touchability when it comes to sex." Rape is a common phenomenon in rural areas. Women are raped as part of caste custom or village tradition. According to Dalit activists, Dalit girls have been forced to have sex with the village landlord. In rural areas, "women are induced into prostitution (*Devadasi system*), which [is] forced on them in the name of religion." The prevalence of rape in villages contributes to the greater incidence of child marriage in those areas. Early marriage between the ages of ten years and sixteen years persists in large part because of Dalit girls' vulnerability to sexual assault by upper-caste men; once a girl is raped, she becomes unmarriageable. An early marriage also gives parents greater control over the caste into which their children are married. Moreover, Dalit women are also raped as a form of retaliation. Landlords and the police use sexual abuse and other forms of violence against women to inflict political "lessons" and crush dissent within the community. One of the reasons that Dalit woman continue to be target of atrocities is that in rural areas, due to extreme poverty, lack of education, and as high caste Hindus own 80% land, Dalit women are forced to work on minimal wage. A slight denial to their orders or daring to ask for a raise in wages can result in humiliations, beating, torture, rape, killing and jail. More often, Dalit womens and children are held by as ransom to catch their spouses on minor charges.

OPPORTUNITIES FOR DALITS IN EDUCATION

The government has made reservations for Dalits, so that they can enter into jobs in the public sector, parliamentary State Assemblies and Universities. This reservation, however, makes them even more vulnerable in the society. Most Dalits continue to live in extreme poverty, without land or opportunities for better employment or education, with the exception of a minority who have benefited from India's policy of quotas in education and government jobs. According to Constitution of India, reservation for Dalits in Government jobs is secured, but in reality, only a few are filled out as they have full control of recruitment. According to the National Commission for SC and ST and as per India's constitution, total job reservation for Dalits is 22.5% but only 2.1% in case of class-I (Dalits serving in pubic commission, civil services, chief executives in major companies) and 9.0% in the case of class-II (this includes Dalits serving as college lecturers, bank manager, in government, etcetera). To date, most Dalit students are prevented from entering in government as well as the public sectors as a part of the caste based discrimination, hence there is a stiff increment in unemployment.

Many brigh Dalit students are prevented from sitting in the front classroom row, sharing water or food, and mixing with high caste students. Teachers are often violent against them for showing greater aptitudes in classrooms. Often humiliated in front of class by the teacher and high caste students, most of those students return back to their family profession. For instance, most recently a Dalit girl student who accidentally joined a street dance performed by high caste performers was humiliated and was threatened with rape if she complained to the police. Turning to the police for a complaint only exaggerated the situation. She later committed suicide.

The Role of International Non-Government Organizations

Now the United Nations and the Human Right groups have exposed the sufferings of these voiceless peoples to the rest of the world. Many Non-Government Organizations (NGO) both in India and as well as abroad have been involved in raising the plight of India's 250 million untouchables. Amongst many, one of the NGOs in North America is called "The Ambedkar Centre for Peace and Justice" (ACJP), named in honour of Dr. B. R. Ambedkar (1891-1956), who was India's foremost human right activist and an untouchable. He has been recognized as the Chief architect of India's Constitution. Dr. Ambedkar was an emancipator, scholar, extraordinaire, social reformer and a true champion of human rights. He was the first Dalits who received a Ph.D. and L.L.D. from Columbia University, USA, D.Sc. and Bar-at-Law from the London School of Economics, and D. Litt. from Osmania University, India. Moreover, he was the first law minister of Independent India.

The most immediate task of the ACJP is to bring the plight of the Dalits to the attention of the International community and to document and publicize human rights abuses. The mission of this organization is to foster recognition of the human rights of, and to develop support for, the indigenous peoples of India. The long-term objectives are to enfranchise Dalits as full citizens of their society. This will require broad-based financial and political support for the Dalits, as well as legal and educational changes in India, so that they may re-establish their dignity, culture and civilization. As warned by the Vice President, Mr. Yogesh Varhade, since fundamentalist Hindu forces are pushing this caste system to the limits, this will result in civil war, instability in South Asia and Global Peace will be in danger. Millions of refugees could infiltrate North America and Europe, further resulting in a complete collapse of the economy, and could cost millions of dollars. The Indian Government is only interested in developing trade with Canada, but does not reveals its "dirty secret" of human rights violations and caste-based atrocities on millions of Dalits. The Canadian government should show compassion to towards dissolving untouchability. For this, Canada should put pressure on the Indian government to recognize untouchabilty as "racial discrimination" and put policies in place to protect human rights and the dignity of million Dalits. Moreover, the Canadian as well as the world media should take an active role in publicizing the plight of Untouchables.

CONCLUSION

In fact, Dalits have been considered the most degraded, downtrodden, exploited and the least educated in Indian society. They are considered to be "*untouchable*" because their touch to high caste people is considered polluted and uncleaned. The caste hierarchy has excluded these people from the caste system and therefore, they are "*outcaste.*" For decades and until today, they have been barred from sharing water, food and shelter and are forced to live in ghettos, and hence are referred as "*segregated.*" They have been socially, culturally, and politically subjugated and marginalized through three thousand years of India's history. What is still surprising is that the Dalits experience the agony of untouchability very deeply in all walks of life: social, economical and political Until today, India's caste system has compelled them to perform the most inhuman jobs, from the manual scavenging, skinning animals, disposal of the dead animals, cleaning streets, landless labour, bonded labour, child labour and performing the most inhuman tasks, such as cleaning the toilet and disposal of human waste.

References

Ambedkar, B.R. *Anhililation of Caste*, New Delhi.

Anant, A. (2003), *Human Rights of Marginal Communities: The Low Caste Dalits In India*. South Asia Partnership of Canada. *India Abroad*. 4 July.

Keer, D. (n.d.), *Dr. Babasaheb Ambedkar*. Bombay, India: Popular Publication.

Moon, V. (1990), *Dr. B. R. Ambedkar, Writings and Speeches*. Vol. 7.

Narula, S. (1998), *"Broken People" Caste Violence against India's Untouchables*. Human Rights Watch.

National Commission for Scheduled Caste and Scheduled Tribes. India, 2000.

O'Neill, T. (2003), "Untouchables." *National Geographic*, 8-31.

Talukdar, S. R. (n.d.), *Merit: The Aryan Bluff*. Bluemoon Books.

Thind, G. S. (n.d.), *Our Indian Sub-Continent Heritage*. Vancouver, BC: Crosstown Press Ltd.

Varhade, Y. (n.d.), *Ambedkar Centre for Peace and Justice*. Tunkhannock, PA, USA.

Viyogi, N. (n.d.), *The Native Culture of India, The Wonder That Was*.

Rothschild, E. (2000), "An Infinity of Girls: The Political Rights of Children in Historical Perspective," Centre for History and Economics, University of Cambridge, UK.

Klot, J.F., and Sowa, T. Graça Machel (2001), The Impact Notes of War on Children, A review of progress since the 1996 United Nations Report on the Impact of Armed Conflict on Children, C. Hurst & Co. (Publishers) Ltd., United Kingdom, (Co-producer UNICEF).

Aravamudan, G. (2007), Disappearing Daughters: The Tragedy of Female Foeticide, Penguin Publishers, New Delhi.

Sen, K.M. and Kumar, S.A.K. (2001), "Women in India–How Free? How Equal?," UNDP-Report Commissioned by the Office of the Resident Coordinator in India.

Karlekar, M. (1995), The Girl Child in India: Does she have any Rights? Canadian Women Studies, March.

Meenakshi Ganguly Thukral (2005), Status of Children in India Inc, HAQ Centre for Child Rights.

Borooah V.K. (2000), "Do Children in India Benefit from having Mothers who are Literate?," This Study is based on Unit Record Data from 1993–94 Human Development Survey Carried out by the National Council of Applied Economic Research, New Delhi, April.

Devaki Jain (2001), "Children's Rights and Women's Rights: Some Connections and Disconnections," *Development*, Vol. 44(2).

Dipak Basu (2000), "Combating Child Labour," *The Hindu*, March 7.

Ganesh, N. (2000), "Child Abuse Stems from Family - A Study: Vulgar Talks, Gestures also Forms of Abuse," *Asian Age*, March 1.

Iftikhar Ahmed (1999), "Getting Rid of Child Labour," *Economic and Political Weekly*, July 3.

Joseph M.P (ed.) (1996), "IPEC in India- 1992–95: Looking Back," International Labour Organisation, International Programme on the Elimination of Child Labour, New Delhi.

Crops Production and Fertilizer Consumption in Tamilnadu: An Impact of Technolory Adoption
(A Micro Level Study)

A. ABDUL RAHEEM* AND C. PRABU**

INTRODUCTION

Agricultural diversification is an important mechanism for economic growth. It depends, however, on there being opportunities for diversification and on farmers' responsiveness to those opportunities. Agricultural diversification can be facilitated by technological breaks-through, by changes in consumer demand or in government policy or in trade arrangements, and by development of irrigation, roads, and other infrastructures. Conversely, it can be impeded by risks in markets and prices and in crop-management practices, by degradation of natural resources, and by conflicting socio-economic requirements - perhaps for employment generation, or for self-sufficiency or foreign-exchange-earning capacity in particular crops or livestock or fishery or forest products.

Agriculture and allied activities constitute the single largest component of India's GDP (gross domestic product), contributing 24% of the total. The importance of this sector to the Indian economy can be gauged by the fact that it provides employment to two-thirds of the total workforce. The share of agricultural products in exports is also substantial, with agriculture accounting for about 15% of export earnings. With a weight of 57% in the consumer price index, food prices

* Assistant Professor and Research Supervisor, Dept. of Economics, The New College, Chennai-14.

** Research Scholar, Dept. of Economics, The New College, Chennai-14 are closely linked with inflation and any adverse shock on agriculture could have cumulative effects on the economy. Agricultural growth also has a direct impact on poverty eradication, and is an important factor in employment generation. The growth of Indian agriculture post-independence and the country's attainment of self-sufficiency in food grains has been an impressive achievement, but it has come at a high ecological cost. Moreover, the challenge is far from over. The food demands of the present and future generations have yet to be met, while the limits of expansion of cultivated land have been reached. Finally, given that almost two-thirds of the net sown area is rain-fed, Indian agriculture continues to be fundamentally dependent on the weather, and hence, highly vulnerable to climate change.

The history of agriculture is the history of intensification. Intensification follows successful innovations. It was innovation in the yields that is Green revolution in the mid-sixties that catalyzed a metamorphosis from the conditions of food shortage to one of self sufficiency and beyond- making India in the process, a world leader in the number of agricultural commodities. Agricultural growth witnessed a sharp turnaround in the immediate post-green revolution phase, largely driven bay the growth in yields. In India, the growth in agricultural output has been largely yield driven with the contribution from marginal acreage being only minimal. Today, while India is a world leader in the production of number of agricultural commodities, its yield levels for most of the crops are nowhere near comparable with what some of the other countries of have achieved. One of the main attributes for the low levels of yield attained in India is the unsatisfactory spread of new technological practices, including cultivation of High Yielding Varieties (HYV).

STATEMENT OF THE PROBLEM

India is developing nation with a strong agricultural base. Agricultural accounts for 22 per cent of the GDP and provides livelihoods to 58 per cent of country's population. Over the years, the agricultural sector has not received as much attention as other sectors in services and manufacturing. It still contributes 4.8% in the total export figure of India. Besides, Indian agriculture is undoubtedly characterized by a very wide diversity in technology employed and there are still past areas covered by traditional agricultural practices with single cropping pattern. Similarly, there are relatively modern and mechanized operations in many states of the country, which also rely on substantial use of fertilizers, pesticides and vast quantities of water. It is seen that the Green revolution took place in Indian agriculture in 1966 made a break through in the practices of agriculture. It made a noticeable shift from area expansion to yield improvement, wherever possible, in order to the meet the growing demand for agricultural products, particularly food. As a consequence of this change, the energy consumption in agricultural sector has increased to increase the size of output. It is pertinent to note that the structure of energy consumption has also changed substantially with a huge shift from animal and human labour towards tractor for farming operations, and electricity and diesel and largely used for groundwater irrigation. It is noted that agriculture by its very nature is an energy conversion process and it is not only a consumer of energy but it is also a producer of energy. In agriculture both commercial and non-commercial energies are used to carryout the agricultural operations. Further, the pattern of energy consumption is intimately linked with the level of mechanization adopted in agricultural operations and has varying requirements of capital/ human labour, animal labour and other biological inputs.

This study aims at analyzing the impact of adoption of technology on crops productivity in Villupuram district of Tamilnadu during the 1995-2005. The impact of technology adoption can be studied in terms of extent of cultivation of high yielding variety of crops, application of NPK fertilizers, application of pesticides and mechanization of agriculture in terms of tractors and power tillers use, and use of machines and equipments in various stages of cultivation of crops. The impact of technology adoption could be learnt in terms of yield per acre of the selected crops. An attempt is made to this study the impact of adoption of technology particularly fertilizer consumption on crops productivity in the study area during reference period.

Identification of the Problem

It may be observed that various sources of energy are used in agriculture from seedbed preparation to transportation of grains. Yet, it uses energy sources in the form of human labour, animal labour, diesel engine, electric motor, power tiller, tractor, seed, fertilizer, farm yard manure, pesticide, agricultural waste, solar power and wind energy. But the source wise energy consumption varies between the areas and dry land and wetland agriculture and among the crops cultivated in particular regions. Despite the rapid increase in mechanism that has taken place in Indian agriculture, several operations like seedbed preparation, transportation, weeding, fertilizing, pesticide application, harvesting and threshing are performed by human labour. In view of the observations made above, the present study intends to analyze the impact of adoption of technology on crop productivity with reference to Villupuram District, Tamilnadu. Therefore, this study has taken only the fertilizer consumption level on crop productivity. Moreover, the major crops cultivation in the district is paddy, sugarcane, cotton, gingili, cumbu, ragi, corn, coriander. Among the crops cultivation, paddy and sugarcane are cultivated by and majority of farmers in Villupuram District, Tamilnadu. In view of the above discussions, observed this study examines impact of adoption of technology on crops productivity in the study area during 1995-2005.

METHODOLOGY

This study aims at analyzing the magnitude and extent of adoption of technology on crop productivity in Villupuram district of Tamilnadu during the 1995-2005, the impact of adoption of technology on crop productivity based on secondary data published by Seasons and crop reports. Moreover, this study selected on adoption of technology particularly fertilizer consumption.

Area of Study

Villupuram district has 22 blocks and among them 6 blocks are selected for the purpose of present study. From each block, one special village panchayat is selected for field investigation viz, Chinnasalem, Ulundurpet, Gingee, Sankarapuram, Marakanam and Vikravandi. Among these villages 3 villages record higher yield of crops viz. Ulundurpet, Sankarapuram and Vikravandi and the remaining three-village panchayats record low yield of crops. In order to access the relative performance of farm mechanization and modernization, these villages are selected. The special villages Panchayats receive special grants and subsidies for farm technology; it is a major reason for selection of these villages.

Data Collection

The secondary data relating to crops productivity and adoption of technology in Villupuram District were collected from published sources from Season and crop Reports: 1995-2004. This study also selected two crops namely Paddy and Sugarcane. Moreover, this study selected on adoption of technology particularly fertilizer consumption. The collected secondary data are analysed by applying appropriate statistical and Mathematical techniques viz., Least square exponential techniques, Mean Co Variance, Multiple Regression and Correlation technique.

ANALYSIS OF DATA AND RESULTS

In order to study trends in fertilizer comsumption in Villupuram District during 1995-2004, the Mean Co Variance and Least Square exponential techniques are applied.

The Mean Co variance is written as:

Mean $(X) = \Sigma X/n$

X = Fertilizer consumption

N = number of year

$C.V = \sigma/X \times 100$

σ = Standard deviation

X = Mean value of fertilizer consumption

The Least Square Exponential model is written as:

$$Y = abx \quad (1)$$

Using the logarithmic equation

$$LogY = logA + XlogB \quad (2)$$

Exponential growth rates (%) have been calculated by the formula

$$\text{Growth Rate} = \text{Antilog } (logb\text{-}1) \times 100 \quad (3)$$

Where,

$$LogB = N\Sigma XlogY - (\Sigma logY)^2/N\Sigma X^2 - (\Sigma X)^2$$

The Multiple Linear Regression Model is written as

$$Y = a + bx_1 + bx_2 + \ldots\ldots bx_8$$

Y = Dependent Variable (year)

$X_1..X_8$ = Independent Variables (i.e., X_1= Gross irrigated area, X_2 = net area irrigated, X_3 = gross are sown, X_4 = Total NPK consumption, X_5 = per hectare NPK consumption, X_6 = total cereals production, X_7 = total pulses production and X_8 = total food grain production)

The Correlation analysis is written as

$$r = \Sigma dxdy - n(X\text{-}A1)\,(Y\text{-}A2) \;/\; \sigma x\, \sigma Y$$

Where,

X = mean of X series

Y = mean of Y series

$A1$ = assumed mean value of X series

$A2$ = assumed mean value of Y series

$\Sigma dxdy$ = product of deviation from assumed averages

σx = Standard deviation of X series

σy = standard deviation of Y series

N = number of pairs

By applying above cited techniques, data presented in Table 1 and 2 Data indicates the area irrigated and the trends in fertilizer consumption in Villupuram district. The gross irrigated area was 504 thousand hectare in 1995-1996, and it rose to 547 thousand hectares in 2004-2005 showing 1.42 per cent of annual growth rate. In the same period net irrigated area has shown 26.40 per cent in the case of gross sown area. The total NPK fertilizer consumption was 126 thousand tonnes in 1995-1996, and it rose to 133 thousand tonnes in 2004-2005 indicating 10.66 per cent of negative growth rate in the period of analysis with the co-efficient of variation of 38.02 per cent. However, per hectare fertilizer consumption shows 2.34 per cent of growth rate in the same period.

Table 1

Area Irrigated and Trends in Fertilizer Consumption in Villupuram District

Year	*Gross Irrigated Area (000) Hectares*	*Net area irrigated (000) Hectares*	*Gross Area Sown*	*Total NPK Consumption*	*Per Hectare NPK Consumption (kg)*
1995-1996	504	443	754	126	168
1996-1997	528	452	763	119	158
1997-1998	575	451	779	120	199
1998-1999	565	447	722	102	204
1999-2000	569	447	757	124	218
2000-2001	516	434	678	116	212
2001-2002	501	438	679	93	112
2002-2003	541	447	726	108	220
2003-2004	543	446	716	107	144
2004-2005	547	448	767	133	227
Mean	538.9	445.3	734.1	114.6	186
SD	26.40	5.57	35.86	12.17	38.72
CV	4.64	1.25	4.88	10.60	20.82
GR	1.42	(-) 26.40	(-) 7.04	(-) 10.53	2.34

Source: Director, Department of Economics and Statistic, Chennai-6, Fertilizer Association of India, New Delhi.

Table 2
Multiple Regressions between Explanatory Variables and Level of Fertilizer

Variables	*Co-efficient*	*Standard error*	*t value*
Constant	643.2138	323.5657	1.9878^{Ns}
Price	0.0006	0.0013	0.4440 ^{Ns}
Gross Irrigated Area	-0.0332	0.1647	-02019^{Ns}
Net irrigated Area	-2.0788	0.9242	-2.2492**
Gross Sown Area	0.5533	0.1275	4.3400**
R^2	0.823		
F ratio	5.84		

Sources: Computed
NS = Not Significant ** Significant at 5 per cent level.

An analysis of multiple regressions expounds the following facts (Table 2). The chosen independent variables such as fertilizer price, gross irrigated area, net irrigated, and gross sown area re found to be statistically significant in their influence of fertilizer consumption. It is evident that the value of R^2 is 0.82, which is significant in terms of the F ratio at 5 per cent level of significance with 4:9 Degrees of freedom. The remaining of 18 per cent of total variation may be attributed to other factors, which are not including in the given model. The regression co-efficient such as, fertilizer price, gross irrigated area, and net irrigated area are not statistically significant in their individual influence on fertilizers consumption. However, gross sown area has a positive individual influence on fertilizer consumption as per the result of t test.

Moreover, Table 3 indicates the production of crops in relation to the fertilizer consumption level in Villupuram district. The total cereals production was 1406 thousand tonnes in 1995-96 and it rose to 1693 thousand tonnes in 2004-2005 showing 0.35 per cent of negative growth rate in the period of analysis with the fluctuation of 108.99 per cent as per the result of co-efficient of variation analysis. In the same period pulses production shows 20.38 per cent of negative growth rate.
The total food grain production was 1472 thousand tonnes in 1995-1996 and it has increased to 1737 thousand tonnes in 2004-2005 indicating 0.37 per cent of negative growth rate in the period of analysis with the fluctuation of 108.40 per cent as per the result of Co-efficient of variation analysis. In the same period total NPK fertilizer consumption has shown 5.55 per cent of increase and there is 35 11 per cent of increase in the case of per hectare consumption of total NPK fertilizer consumption.

Table 3
The Production Crops and Fertilizer Consumption in Villupuram District

				NPKConsumption	
Year	*Total Cereals Production ('000 he)*	*Total Pulses Production ('000 hec)*	*Total Food grain Production ('000 hec)*	*Total '000 tonnes*	*Per he (Kg/hec)*
1995-1996	1406	65.4	1472	126	168
1996-1997	1577	80.8	1658	119	156
1997-1998	1758	52.8	1810	120	199
1998-1999	1140	24.8	1164	102	204
1999-2000	1845	55.1	1900	124	218
2000-2001	1206	23.9	1229	116	212
2001-2002	907	25.7	932	93	112
2002-2003	1045	32.1	1077	108	220
2003-2004	1512	51.3	1563	107	144
2004-2005	1963	44.1	1737	133	227
Mean	1408.9	45.6	1454.2	114.6	186
SD	321.36	19.11	334.81	12.17	38.72
C V	108.99	42.02	108.40	9.93	20.82
GR	(-) 0.35	(-) 20.38	(-) 0.37	5.55	35.11

Source: Director, Department of Economics and Statistic, Chennai - 6, Fertilizer Association of India, New Delhi.

The correlation test is applied for further discussion, Table 4 indicates that the computed correlation between total cereals production and fertilizer consumption is 0.32, which implies low degree of negative correlation between total cereals production and fertilizer consumption level. A similar result has been observed with respect to total food grain production and fertilizer consumption level. However, a low degree of correlation (-0.18) has been observed between total pulses production and fertilizers consumption level.

Table 4
Correlation between Crops Production and Fertilizer Consumption

Variables	*Correlation(r)*
Total Cereals Production Vs Fertilizer Consumption	0.3167
Total Pulses Production Vs Fertilizer Consumption	-0. 1862
Total Food grain Production Vs Fertilizer Consumption	0.2933

Source: Computed.

CONCLUSION

It could be deducted from above discussion that in Villupuram district, a slight shortfall is noticed in net area irrigated and total level of fertilizer consumption. However, an increasing trend in fertilizers consumption and irrigated gross are has been observed. It is also concluded that total food grain production shows less than 1 per cent of negative growth rate in Villupuram district during the study. But, the fertilizer consumption level shows positive growth rate; however the degree of correlation is positive between the total cereals production and fertilizer consumption level.

References

Alagumani, T. (1998), "Energy Use for Corp Production in Uthamapalayam Block, Madurai District, Tamil Nadu", *Indian Journal of Agricultural Economics,* 53(3), July-September, 292-3.

Amarjit Singh and A.J. Singh (1996), "Energy Consumption Pattern in Punjab Agriculture: Inter-size and Inter Regional variations", *Energy Management,* 20(3), July, 31-37.

Ashok Chamotra, T.V. Moorti and Bhim Singh (1976), "Bullock Energy Input for Selected Crops in Paonta Valley of Himachal Pradesh", *Indian Journal of Agricultural Economics,* 31(3), July-September, 241.

Bhatia Ramesh (1977), "Energy and Rural Development in India: Some Issues, *Agricultural and Energy.*

Bhatia, R.C., R. S. Bawa, Satindort and Dalbir Sing Saskaria (1992), "Energy Use Pattern in Punjab Agriculture", *Agricultural Situation in India,* (17 (9), December, 699-703.

Bhagttacharyya Saumyendra (1994), "Optimal Fuelmix in Rural Economy: A Village Level Exercise", *Economic and Political Weekly,* 29(25), 1529-36.

Chatterijee, P.K. and Shibdas Benerjee (1976), "Energy Requirements in Paddy Cultivation-A Study of Selected Farms in West Bengal", *Indian Journal of Agricultural Economics,* 31(3), July-September, 248-49.

Deva Senapathy, P., K.R. Swaminathan, V. Murugesan, C. Ratnam and R. Balasubramaniam (1989), "Bio-Energy for Agriculture", *Indian Journal of Agricultural Engineering, ISAF,* 26(3).

Dhawan, K.C. and J. P. Mittal (1990), "Energy Scenario of Paddy and Wheat Production in Indian", *Journal of Rural Development,* 9(4), 719-728.

Garg, J. S., G. N. Singh and K. N. Pandey (1976), "An Estimation of Energy Requirements on Mechanized Farms in District Muzaffer Nagar, Uttar Pradesh, *Indian Journal of Agricultural Economics,* (3), July- September, 247.

Giriappa, S. (1986), "Share of Sector wise Energy Consumption in India", *Southern Economist,* September 1, 11-13.

Gordon Sloggett (1974), "Energy used for Pumping Irrigation Water in the United States", *Agriculture and Energy.*

Goswami, H.G. (1976), "Energy Requirement for Lift Irrigation in Taraj Area of North Bihar", *Indian Journal of Agricultural Economics,* 31(3), July-September, 248.

Indiramani and J.S. Panwar (1993), "Requirement of Energy and Power for Diferet Tillage Implements at Part-load Settings", *Indian Journal of Agricultural Engineering,* 3(3:4).

James R. Gilley and Darrel G. Watts (1977), "Energy Reduction Through Improved Irrigation Practices", *Agricultural and Energy,* 187-203.

Joseph R. Barse (1977), "Agriculture and Energy Use in the Year 2000: Discussion from a Natural Resource Perspective", *American Journal of Agricultural Economics,* 59(5), December, 1073-74.

Kulshreshtha, S.P., Brijendra Singh and L.R. Singh, "Energy Requirement for Paddy Crop on Three Sizes of Farms.

Globalization, Urbanization and Urban Environment: An Issue and Challenges

A. ABDUL RAHEEM*, ABDUS SHUKUR** AND M. ABDUL JAMAL***

INTRODUCTION

Urbanization has been the dominant demographic trend, not only in the Asia-Pacific region, but also in the entire world, during the last half century. With the high pace of social and economic development in Asia and the resulting growth of city and town population, lack of infrastructure, congested traffic, environmental degradation and a housing shortage became the major issues faced by cities and towns in their sustainable development. The Asia-Pacific Forum for Environment and Development (APFED) reviewed the environment and development issues facing in the Asia-Pacific Region and identified five major issues that require priority attention. Based on discussions at the past two substantive sessions, APFED formulated its Recommendations and a Message to the World Summit on Sustainable Development (WSSD, in which APFED committed to launch the new partnership initiatives. One of the topics that APFED attaches high importance and is therefore covered by its Recommendations is Urbanization. APFED recommended taking an integrated approach to manage urbanization and strengthen local initiatives in the management of urban environment. APFED, however, has not discussed the urbanization in a comprehensive and detailed manner. According to the prior consultation among APFED members and advisors, the primary focus of the present expert group meeting is set for systematic and better management of urbanization through

* Assistant Professors (SG), Dept. of Economics, The New College, Chennai-14.
** Assistant Professor (SS), Dept of Economics, The New College, Chennai-14.
*** Assistant Professor, Dept of Economics, The New College, Chennai-14.

sustainable land use policies and tools, taking into account thematic coherence with the preceding session focusing on rural land management. Hence, issues concerning the intra-urban management of the environmental quality and human health, as well as development of specific infrastructure and services are a bit outside our scope. These issues have been extensively discussed in other forum, such as the he Ministerial Conference on Environment and Development in Asia and the Pacific 2000 and the World Summit on Sustainable Development (WSSD) Local Government Session. Therefore this paper has been discussed issues and challenges of globalization, urbanization and urban environment in Asia Pacific Region.

Globalization and Process

Globalization is a set of economic processes in which production, marketing and investment are integrated across the borders of nations. The liberalization and opening up of markets to the global economy is leading to the emergence of a single market for goods, capital, technology, services, and information and to some extent labour. Globalization is also a socio–political process because of its impact on culture, governance and domestic policy. The process of globalization is a convergence, though at differing speeds, of many institutional, legal, economic, social and cultural practices and processes across the borders of nations. Globalization as an idea is how we looking at the world and reducing cultural diversity in terms of perceptions and products. The logic of globalization is the expansion of trade and investment in search of new markets and more competitive production sites. Companies The current tendency of Multi-National Companies (MNC's) or Trans National Companies (TNC's) to relocate geographically and set up production units in other areas of the world with cheaper labour, more lenient health and safety requirements, lower environmental protection standards and favourable tax laws in order to maximize profits. The rising power of MNC's is skewing the distribution of gains towards the corporations, undermining the authority of national government and civil society, eroding human rights and environmental protection and also influencing the proliferating laws governing trade and investment. Globalization trends create challenges on a scale and scope and speed unprecedented in World History. Particularly for developing countries, the challenges are increasingly complex to negotiate because they impact across the sectors and at many levels of society. The challenge for policy makers at the different levels of government is to articulate with the global economy so as to harness the potential benefits for national development and minimize the negative effects, as the global trade system has led to increased environmental damage and violation of human rights. For the developme nt planners, the challenge is to address the effects of rapid expansion of corporate interests. Measures to protect ecological stability for local communities against the benefits of corporate operation i.e. measures that promote the sustainable use of the environment. The process of globalization and the global changes affects the development of the cities. Cities comprise a paradox. They embody the leading centers of development but they are also a fertile soil for social exclusions and environmental problems.

ENVIRONMENTAL CHALLENGES UNDER GLOBALIZATION

Globalization generates new challenges in preparing strategies for urban development because globalization threatens to exacerbate urban environmental pollution and natural resource degradation. The strategy is to make cities livable, provide environmental services for the urban people and protect urban people against environmental hazards.

- The concept of the livable city is defined in terms of a healthy and dignified living environment i.e. addressing the sources of environmental degradation.
- The environmental services for the urban people are to provide cleaner air, cleaner water and healthier cities.
- Protect urban people against urban environmental insults and hazards like global warming, ozone depletion etc.

Urban environment encompasses the interaction of population, growth, city management and the built environment with the natural environment or ecological system in which city is located. Urban environment also links other parameters of the urban puzzle like health, energy, infrastructure and land use. A fundamental dimension of sustainable development is sustaining the growth and development of the city while balancing the benefits with complex ecological systems and the global environment.

Urban Environmental Issues and Challenges

Urban environmental problems are threats to people's present or future wellbeing, resulting in human induced damage to the physical environment in or borne into urban areas. Urban environmental issues are raised by urban development initiatives and are related to environmental problems. They are:

- Localized environmental health problems like inadequate potable water and sanitation facilities, indoor air pollution and excessive crowding
- City regional environmental problems like ambient air pollution, inadequate and inefficient waste disposal management, pollution of water bodies and loss of green areas.
- Extra urban impacts of urban activities like ecological disruption and resource depletion and emission of chemicals and green house gases.
- The urban impacts of regional or global environmental burden that may arise from activities outside the city's geographical boundaries, but will affect people living in the city.
- The following table presents a wide range of urban environmental problems. Better urban practices and governance could help to reduce these environmental problems.

There is a number of emerging environmental challenges that cities will need to address. They are as follows: (i) Providing basic environmental services in a way that most effectively protects health (a) Access to safe potable water, sanitation and drainage facilities (b) Proper management of solid waste collection and disposal (c) Reduction of pollution within the households by providing cleaner fuel for cooking and improved household ventilation. (ii) Identification and implementing integrated approaches to urban environment to prevent and abate the impacts of pollution and degradation (a) Ambient air pollution (b) Surface water pollution (c) Ground water pollution and depletion (d) Land use and ecosystem degradation (iii) Proper dealing with accidents and environmental disasters deriving from both natural and man made efforts. Some of the worst sites of ecological disaster are found in and around cities (iv) Urban poverty and environmental conditions are interrelated. This poverty is exacerbated by environmental threats that account for a large share of ill health, early death and hardships to human beings (v) Urban environmental factors are affecting human health, particularly in the field of fertility. In some countries, sperm counts are drastically reduced (vi) 6. Understanding the influence of urbanization on food system i.e. food supply, marketing and distribution vi) Urban sprawl. The population is increasing in urban areas, leading to the decline in the amount of open space available and urban poor will take up illegal residence on the periphery of the city. These settlements become slums of the most appalling nature and adversely affect the environment viii) Urban consumption and production patterns are the root cause or main culprit of environmental deterioration. Therefore better urban environmental management is required.

With this backdrop of urban environmental issues and challenges, globalization generates new challenges in preparing strategies for urban development. The effects of globalization will profoundly affect the future development of the urban centers and cities. Therefore, it could be note that the Use the forces of globalization constructively by assessing the local potential and integrating this into strategies for urban development and co-ordinate strategies for urban development and support partnership between public, private and NGO's. Use regional and urban identities in adapting to global change. Develop innovative and sustainable long-term perspectives in which cities potential strength's are linked to regional competence and culture and use the global trends to shape the urban environment. 6. Good urban governance and management is required in view of globalization. The silver lining is that the increased pace of urbanization and its linkages to economic globalization have reinvigorated interest in good urban governance and management and its links to economic growth. Good urban governance and management is one of the main pillars of sustainable cities. Good governance is primarily through community participation, private sector involvement & NGO's action. Appropriate policy design, decision making, prompt monitoring and evaluation have all relied on networking among the various stakeholders in the urban environment field. The combined efforts of economic, social, political, cultural and ethical factors to define the fundamental of good governance i.e. fiscal discipline, fair and transparent resource allocation, effective and predictable regulatory system, independent and just mechanism for conflict resolution, strategic planning, fiduciary responsibility, participatory decision making, safety and security for all, open information flows and ethical behaviour. The good governance in the backdrop of effects of globalization on urban environmental involves:

- Provision for basic environmental services like sanitation, solid waste collection and disposal management.
- Provision for better environmental management like preventing ecosystem degradation, ozone depletion.
- Improving environmental quality - by imposing emission charges on pollution.

- Provision for environmental justice like access to clean air & water.
- Specific laws to deal with environmental deterioration.
- Effective tools to protect urban poor against global market hazards.
- Community involvement becomes more critical to effectively deal with environmental problems.

  Capacity building initiatives to enable all levels of government and other stakeholders to implement responsive and sustainable programmes.

Conclude by stating that world is urbanizing and will continue to do so and preventing urbanization is neither possible nor desirable. So what is required is better urban environmental governance and management in view of globalization.

Urbanization – An Ongoing Process

Over the past half century, a great rural-to-urban population shift has occurred and the process of urbanization (the concentration of people and activities into areas classified as urban) is set to continue well into the 21st century. Major demographic evidence has indicated that already the Asia-Pacific region is well advanced in the transition from predominantly rural to predominantly urban societies. Although population growth rates have slowed down in many countries for the past decade, 62 per cent of the world' population will live in urban areas by the year 2020, while the Asia-Pacific Region will contain about 49 per cent of that urban population and will have contained a level of urbanization of 55 per cent. An additional 1.2 billion people will be living in the urban centers of the Asia- Pacific region by 2020. It is projected that some of the big countries of the region like China, Indonesia and Pakistan where current urbanization levels are below 50 per cent, will cross this figure by the next quarter of the century. In 1990, seven of the world's fourteen megacities were located in the region rose to nine and it is predicted that there would be eleven - twelve megacities in the region by early 2000. There is a strong positive link between national levels of human development and urbanization levels, while cities spearhead their countries' economic development, transforming society through extraordinary growth in the productivity of labour and promising to liberate the masses from poverty, hunger, disease and premature death. However, the implications of rapid urban growth include increasing unemployment, lack of urban services, overburdening of existing infrastructure and lack of access to land, finance and adequate shelter, increasing violent crime and sexually transmitted diseases, and environmental degradation. Even as national output is rising, a decline in the quality of life for a majority of population that offsets the benefit of national economic growth is often witnessed. Urbanization thus imposes significant burden to sustainable development.

PROBLEM FOCUS - CHALLENGES OF URBANIZATION

Environmental Implications

It should be noted that urban growth has a number of positive impacts on the environment and human well-being, i.e. higher population densities man lower per capita costs of providing energy, health care, infrastructure and services. Also, urbanization has historically been associated with declining birth rates, which reduces population pressure on land and natural resources. Despite all these positive impacts, almost all major cities of the region are increasingly plagued by environmental problems. Some major aspects are as follows:

(a) As a direct result of urbanization, great threat to health and safety in cities comes from water and air pollution, especially at the households and community levels. While ambient air pollution impairs the health of almost all urban residents in many cities, indoor air pollution is particularly hazardous for women and children of low-income households who are regularly exposed to higher concentrations of air pollutants from cooking and heating sources in poorly-ventilated housing. Waterborne diseases are found most commonly in low-income neighborhoods as a result of inadequate sanitation, Drainage and solid waste collection services, health risks, especially to the poor, are also posed by pesticides and industrial effluents.

(b) The productivity of many cities is adversely affected by traffic congestion and water pollution. The loss in productivity includes the total productive time wasted in and the associated increase in the costs of operating and maintaining vehicles. The rising costs of treating polluted water for industrial and domestic purposes are damaging the productivity of urban economies. Fisheries are also being severely harmed by water pollution.

(c) Uncollected and improperly handled solid waste can have serious health consequences. They block drainage systems and contaminate groundwater at landfill sites. In many cities, particularly those in Pacific island countries, it is difficult to secure land for waste disposal facilities, especially onshore landfill sites. Most cities in the region are also unable to manage the increasing amounts of hazardous wastes generated by rapid industrialization.

(d) Conversion of agricultural land and forest, as well as reclaiming of wetlands, for urban uses and infrastructure, are associated with widespread removal of vegetation to support urban ecosystem and put additional pressure on nearby areas that may be even more ecologically sensitive. Groundwater overdraft has led to land subsidence and a higher frequency of flooding, particularly in the lowest-lying and poorest areas.

(e) Urbanization in coastal areas often leads to the destruction of sensitive ecosystems and can also alter the hydrology of coasts and their natural features such as mangrove swamps, reefs and beaches that serve as barriers to erosion and form important habitats for species.

Urbanization does not have only local environmental impacts but also large so-called 'ecological footprints' beyond their immediate vicinity. Intensive and extensive exploitation of natural resources to support urban economy includes excessive extraction of energy resources (including fuel wood), quarrying and excavation of sand, gravel and building materials at large scales, and overextraction of water. These all contribute to degradation of the natural support systems and irreversible loss of critical ecosystem functions, such as the hydrological cycle, carbon cycle and biological diversity, in addition to conflicts with rural uses of such limited resources. Other effects can be felt further afield such as pollution of waterways, long-range air pollution that impact on human health as well as on vegetation and soils at a considerable distance.

Poverty

The growth of large cities, particularly in developing countries, has been accompanied by an increase in urban poverty which tends to be concentrated in certain social groups and in particular locations. Pollution especially affects the poor live at the urban periphery, where manufacturing and processing plants are built and where environmental protection is frequently weak. Environmental sensitive sites such as steep hillsides, flood plains, dry land or the most polluted sites near solid waste dumps and next to open drains and sewers are often the only places where low-income groups can live without the fear of eviction. The poorest groups thus suffer the most from the floods, landslides or other disasters that increasingly batter the cities of developing countries.

Waste Recycling-New Challenges of Sustainability

Waste generation in urban areas continues to increase world-wide in tandem with concentration of populations and increase in living standards, and has reached to unmanageable levels in many localities. High proportion of the waste could be recycled, not simply to reduce the amount of waste to be disposed of. The practice also provides an opportunity to generate income for the urban poor, to prevent environmental damages of waste dumping, and further to demonstrate less material- and energy-intensive consumption patterns. Promotion of sustainable consumption should have the far-reaching benefit of fostering domestic enterprises and pushing the production sector towards sustainable pathways. There is a need to develop an integrated approach where the public, private and community sectors work together to develop local solutions promoting sustainable waste management of material recycling.

CAUSAL FACTORS BEHIND URBANIZATION

General: The major reasons for increasing urban population are rural to urban migration, including international migration to a lesser extent, and the re-classification or expansion of existing city boundaries to include populations that were hitherto classified as being resident outside the city limits. These are estimated to contribute about 60 per cent of the region's urban growth, while natural increase counts for some 40 per cent.3

Rural -Urban Migration: Primary driving forces of rural-urban migration include the opportunities and services offered in urban areas—especially jobs and education, while in some cases, conflict, land degradation and exhaustion of natural resources in rural areas are also important. The patterns of rural-urban migration may be city-specific, reflecting, among other things, changes in the city's economic base, labour market and age structure. They also reflect social, economic and political changes within the region and nation and are influenced by economic factors in the surrounding and distant rural areas, such as landowning structure, agricultural practices and crop prices, and overall rural productivity. Most evidence suggests that increasing the income and level of education of rural populations accelerates migration and this phenomenon, coupled with the greater access to urban areas, has led to an inevitable increase in rural populations seeking employment opportunities in urban areas.

Links to Globalization: The steady increase in the level of urbanization reflects the fact that the size of the world's economy has grown many times and has also changed from one dominated by relatively closed national economies or trading blocs to one where most countries have more open economies and where production and the services it needs, including financial services, are increasingly integrated internationally. These trends appear to be strengthening, reinforced especially by the freer and faster flows of information and knowledge under the impact of new information technologies. Technology has increased the already dominant economic role and importance of urban areas worldwide, indicating the growing importance of cities in the global economy.

Mismanagement: It is often pointed out that many urban environmental problems are the result of poor management, poor planning and absence of coherent urban policies rather than of urbanization itself. The problem of urbanization has significantly been exacerbated by inappropriate incentive systems, such as the "growth-first" strategy adopted by the Governments of many countries in the region, especially in developing countries. In order to attract investment, industrial promotion policies are designed to offer privileges and incentive packages, including low-taxes lax regulations and subsidized infrastructure with target to urban areas. Industrial growth, combined with inadequate infrastructure, inappropriate pricing of resources and services, and inadequate institutional mechanism to ensure environmental protection, further accelerates environmental degradation in urban areas. The 'land market' factors that accounted for exacerbating urbanization problems include inappropriate regulation, lack of tenure security, inadequate infrastructure capacity inadequate information, inadequate pricing and taxation, and weak institutions and poorly coordinated actors in the land market. All these factors necessitate significant improvements in overall urban governance to effectively reduce and bypass the urbanization problems.

Policy Responses and Tools to manage Urbanization: A variety of options in terms of policy responses and tools to cope effectively with the urbanization transition has been proposed and discussed for several decades. These options may be categorized in the following four strategic steps.

(a) National planning to control urbanization to manageable levels: In an attempt to ensure better management of urbanization, Governments have had adopted macroeconomic policies that are designed to mitigate magnitude of urbanization to manageable levels, or to keep people in rural areas. As a primary tool, a National Physical (Spatial) Development Plan could be established to address the mid- and long-term national direction on distribution of population; utilization of land; development of new land, water and energy; provision of infrastructure, housing and transportation that favor decentralized economic development. Such planning approach, especially when coordinated with the overall economic policy as well as relevant sectoral development programmers covering, in particular, industrial and agricultural productivity, would be effective in establishing an orderly and consistent utilization of land on a national basis and providing the opportunity for urbanization issues to be addressed in the coherent way in the context of overall national development.

(b) Regional and Urban Land Use Planning to Guide Urbanization: Following the provisions set by the national development plan, land-use planning and management tools at regional (sub-national, provincial) and urban local levels have long been expected to play a crucial role in avoiding and mitigating the adverse impacts of rapid, unplanned urbanization. Regional planning tools for the purpose include the planned development of intermediate urban centers, promotion of polycentric regional network of urban centres, and economic development of smaller towns and cities in less concentrated areas in rural provinces. At the city level, local governments have been encouraged to carry out an integrated land-use planning to comprehensively address adverse impacts of urbanization, including environmental problems. Zoning techniques, which may be applied to implement the master plan and to guide urban development to spatially appropriate areas, include designation of sensitive land resources and areas, establishment of buffer zones, management of hazard-prone lands, protection of cultural resources, conservation of open spaces and urban green, management of prime agricultural land, guiding and discouraging of excessive urban sprawl. Regulatory instruments such as land and household registration/information systems, property tax systems, land tenure systems, and building and land development permits are all important basic tools that can be strengthened for effectively implementing spatial planning and zoning techniques. Compact development techniques such as 'smart growth' movement and sustainable city initiatives have been advocated to

combat urban sprawl, promoting the build-up within an already urbanized area, redeveloping on cleaned-up contaminated sites or 'brownfields', and cluster development on reduced-size lots.

As a reaction to the shortcomings of traditional planning approaches, and more recently to address the needs of sustainable development, various countries have adopted new processes and approaches to urban planning. *Action planning* is a 'learning by doing' approach to resolve urbanization problems in a short term perspective, with minimum data collection and planning procedures. Local community participation in decision-making is deemed a key to success. *Strategic planning* is also a participatory approach to integrated urban development to achieve growth management and remedial actions at both the city-wide and community scales. The output of the process is not just a physical development plan but a set of inter-related strategies for city development covering land, infrastructure, finance and institutions. There are a number of technical tools which are now becoming widely used as part of effective urban planning approaches. Amongst others, *Geographical information systems (GIS)* are gaining increasing importance as a tool for decision-making in planning. The essence of GIS is to link together different data sets and present them clearly and concisely in a variety of ways. GIS can also aid short-staffed local governments in better managing rapid urban growth. *Land market assessments* provides accurate and up-to date information on land prices, supply of serviced land, present and future land projects, housing typologies, and other aspects of the housing and land market, and thus is used to support government planning and decision making, the evaluation of government policies and actions, Private sector investment and development decisions and structuring of land based taxation systems. There are also a number of improved zoning techniques, such as mixed zoning, floating zoning, conditional or contract zoning and phased zoning.

Both rational decision-making regarding overall policies and implementing specific programmes to effectively address urbanization requires a sense of comparative risks. Environmental and socio-economic impact assessment and risk ranking are useful planning tools for this purpose. In addition to traditional zoning procedures, new techniques such as strategic environmental assessment are being adopted, as a means of integrating potential environmental considerations at the early stages of strategic policy formulation.

(c) Intra-urban management to cope with urbanization problems : Despite all the policy responses to better manage the urbanization, as

outlined in (a) and (b) above, the chances to prevent the urbanization transition would still be slim from practical point of view. Then, the challenge to many city managers still remains as to project and build the necessary infrastructure and services (housing, public transport; and sewage, water supply, and waste disposal systems) outpacing the wave of rural-urban migrants suffocate the existing urban agglomerations. Investment requirements of urban infrastructure in Asia and the Pacific are massive and impose enormous demands on fiscal resources. As a number of financial options has been proposed and experimented in the region, the range of such options is certainly expanding with the region-wide trend of providing local governments with greater discretion in the levying of taxes, fees and service charges, and of increased reliance on the private sector.

Provision of infrastructure should not be seen merely as a reactive response to ongoing urbanization, often a curative measure to deteriorating urban environment. It could rather be used as a guide to future urban build-up in more positive way, to guide it to spatially more appropriate areas. Among other infrastructure sectors, urban transport system could play a crucial role in this context. Technical options include advance planning, stepwise/strategic introduction of mass transit system, and aggressive use of congestion pricing. Because of the importance of specific local circumstances and political realities, there is no viable approach to solving urban environmental problems that can be applied in every city. A basic step is to develop a local environmental agenda to assess the local situation regarding environmental issues so that this information can be integrated in urban planning. The process involves routinely incorporating environmental information and data, standards and policy targets, techniques and monitoring in strategic urban development plans. Spatial, cross-media, inter-temporal factors must all be taken into consideration. Successful urban environmental management may include the following sectoral elements, increases in resource efficiency, reductions in waste generation, improving urban infrastructure for water supply, the management and conservation of water resources in urban areas by improved waste water treatment and through legislation, setting up of recycling schemes, development of more effective waste collection systems, strict legislation for the treatment of hazardous waste, waste collection through public-private partnership, adoption of energy technologies by industry and households, and restoration of brownfields.

(d) Participation, Partnership and Governance: Through experience, it has been learned that no amount of finance, technology or expertise can secure environmentally sustainable urban development—or protect the environment—if the fundamentals of governance are not participatory, democratic and pluralistic. Many developing countries have developed extensive regulations on pollution, most of which are not applied effectively because of the lack of proper institutions, legal systems, political will and competent governance. Unfortunately, particularly where economic and social change is rapid, established political and administrative institutions have proved highly resistant to change.

Improving the urban governance, in particular, through increasing transparency and accountability of policy formulation and decision making processes, is a key to success in implementing any urban management policies and plans. Participation of all stakeholders who are benefiting from relevant decisions and actions should be ensured at all levels of planning activities, in combination with greater access to relevant information and enhancement of public awareness of urbanization issues. Efforts to improve urban governance essentially involve activities promoting participatory processes; developing effective partnerships with and among all actors of civil society, particularly the private and community sectors; securing greater effective empowerment of local government, including greater autonomy in finance and legislation; and reform of unresponsive organizations and bureaucratic structures.

(e) Efforts by Countries of the Asia-Pacific Region: A number of countries in the region have attempted to develop greater integration in their development and environmental policy making to manage urbanization. Japan provides rich experiences of successive applications of the National Land Development Plan and the Capital Region Development Improvement Plans as basic planning tools at the national scale, and operations of the Regional Environmental Pollution Control Program (REPCP) at the regional level. Examples of systematic consideration of broader issues of metropolitan scale land management, infrastructure investment, financing mechanisms and governance in an integrated manner, include the Klang Valley Environmental Plan in Malaysia and the Ho Chi Minh City Environmental Planning Project in Viet Nam. Within improved urban land management systems, various integrated planning and regulatory systems are now linked to institutional, sectoral investment and fiscal policies. Planning and regulatory tools are also being improved, such as the "broad brush",

structure planning approaches used in the JABOTABEK Metropolitan Development Plan in Indonesia and the Metro Manila Capital Investment Folio in the Philippines.

CONCLUSION

Over the last few decades, many cities in the region have experimented with the development of neighborhood or community organizations to ensure that equity and social issues are properly addressed in the local governance processes. These organizations are consulted on the planning of new development, implementation of infrastructure improvement and implementation of tariff or tax increases. Furthermore, programmes are developed under which community organizations can be responsible for their own infrastructure development, with some notable successes including the delivery of services in sanitation (Karachi), public health (Calcutta) and environmental protection (Metro Manila). The Kampung Improvement Programme in Surabaya, Indonesia is regarded as one of the most successful initiatives to improve housing and living conditions, achieved with households and community organizations making major contributions both to provision and to maintenance of basic infrastructures.

References

United Nations Centre for Human Settlements (HABITAT), *An Urbanizing World - Global Report on Human Settlements 1996*, Oxford University Press 1996.

United Nations Economic and Social Commission for Asia and the Pacific (UN/ESCAP), *"State of Urbanization in Asia and the Pacific 1993"*, United Nations, 1993.

United Nations Economic and Social Commission for Asia and the Pacific (UN/ESCAP), and Asian Development Bank (ADB), *"State of the Environment in Asia and the Pacific 2000"*,

United Nations, 2000 United Nations Environment Programme (UNEP), *"GEO: Global Environment Outlook 3"*, Earthscan Publishing, 2002. *Past, Present and Future Perspectives.*

Metropolitan Environment Improvement Program, *"Japan's Experience in Urban Environmental Management"*, The World Bank and UNDP, 1994.

Hardoy, Mitlin and Stterthwaite (2001), *"Environmental Problems in an Urbanizing World"*, Earthscan Publishing, 2001 Lo and Marcotullio (ed.), *"Globalization and the Sustainability of Cities in the Asia Pacific Region"*, United Nations University Press.

Bernstein (1993), *"Urban Management and the Environment 12 - Land Use Considerations in Urban Environmental Management"*, UNDP/ UNCHS/ World Bank Urban Management Programme.

Women Employment in the Export Processing Zones in India: A Measure for Social Protection

A. ABDUL RAHEEM* AND K. SAMBASIVAM**

INTRODUCTION

The link between export employment and the feminisation of employment is now well known. (See Horton [1995], Wee [1998] and Joekes [1999]). While feminisation of employment can refer to either the absolute or the relative increase in numbers of women employed, most of the literature on this process in export-oriented employment has tended to look at the share of women to total workers in particular sectors. This is because the absolute increase in such employment (or even an increase in the share of women so employed to total female labour force) could be part of a fairly standard development pattern whereby more and more people are drawn into labour markets determined by changing patterns of labour demand, but need not tell us anything about any particular preference for women workers. By contrast, the relative increase in the share of women in total export employment, which was so marked for a period in parts of Asia, is a qualitatively different phenomenon. Of course, such feminisation has obviously been reflected in more and more women being drawn into paid employment.

WOMEN EMPLOYMENT IN EXPORT PROCESSING ZONES (EPZs)

This process was most marked over the period 1980 to 1995 in the high-exporting economies of East and Southeast Asia, where the share

* Research Supervisor and Assistant Professor in Economics, The New College, Chennai-14.
** Associate Professor, Dept. of Economics, Bharathidhasan Govt. College for Women, Pondy-3.

of female employment in total employment in the Export Processing Zones (EPZs) and export-oriented manufacturing industries typically exceeded 70 per cent. It was also observed in a number of other developing countries, for example in Latin America in certain types of export manufacture.

Women workers were preferred by employers in export activities primarily because of the inferior conditions of work and pay that they were usually willing to accept. Thus, women workers had lower reservation wages than their male counterparts, were more willing to accept longer hours and unpleasant and often unhealthy or hazardous factory conditions, typically did not or engage in other forms of collective bargaining to improve conditions, and did not ask for permanent contracts. They were thus easier to hire and fire at will and according to external demand conditions, and also, life cycle changes such as marriage and childbirth could be used as proximate causes to terminate employment.

The most visible sign of the link between feminisation of paid work and export orientation is of course in export processing zones. In India such zones have been both less prominent and less successful than in the Southeast Asian economies, but nevertheless they also bring out the reasons for employers, Preference for female workers of a certain age group as well as the need to ensure minimal employment security in such areas.

The idea of an EPZ - which is also known in other countries of Asia as a Free Trade Zone, Special Economic Zone, and so on, is essentially to provide special incentives to exporters and to allow them to avoid or bypass many of the laws and physical and material constraints which supposedly inhibit export growth in the rest of the economy. As Raman [1989] has pointed out, whatever be the terminology, the significance of the Export Processing Zones lies essentially in its physical, social and economic separation from the rest of the country.. Indeed, the latest Exim policy announced by the Government of India declares that the new term will be Free Trade Zones (FTZ) to replace Export Processing Zones and these are to be treated as outside the country's customs territory.

Export Processing Zone and Women Employment

In India, the first EPZ was established at Kandla in 1960, which was one of the earliest of all developing countries. At present, there are seven EPZs operational within the country, while two more are planned. Of these, the largest three - Santa Cruz EPZ, Noida EPZ and

Madras EPZ - employ the bulk of the workers and account for more than 85 per cent of the exports of all the EPZs out together. However, EPZs themselves are still rather unimportant in quantitative terms: over the 1990s they together accounted for less than 4 per cent of the value of all exports from India, and their share has actually stagnated over the past decade despite the increasing number and value of various economic incentives that have been offered to them.

In aggregate they currently employ around 80,000 directly, but some reports suggest that the extent of indirect and unofficial employment is much larger and may be growing. The three large EPZs account for 80 per cent of all EPZ direct employment according to the official data. However, this includes only those workers who are permanent and are entered on the company record books. There are thousands of other workers, who either do not appear on the company records or may be working as contract workers. Thus, for example, the PRIA [2000] study of EPZs found that in Madras EPZ, the MEPZ workers union which is the only union of EPZ workers in India, did not accept the official total employment figure of the zone of 17,000, but rather put the figure around 36,000-38,000 out of which almost 25,000 are women.

The numerical dominance of women workers is a characteristic feature of EPZs across the world, and the Indian EPZs also follow along the same lines. In both Santa Cruz and Madras EPZs, women workers constituted 70-80 per cent of the work force. NOIDA was somewhat of an exception, with only 30-35 per cent women workers. These women are also typically young - the average age is found to be between 20 and 25 years, with around 10 per cent even younger, in their teens, and only around 1 per cent above the age of 30 years.

Officially, EPZs are also governed by the labour laws of the country, but certain distinctions and loopholes have meant that they are honoured only in the breach. Thus, the law states that union activity is permissible. Work hours as per law have been limited to 48 hours per week. Provident fund contributions by the employer, which are limited to just 8 per cent, become applicable after 3 to 5 years. The Bonus law prescribes a minimum of 8.33% and maximum of 20%, which however, is not obligatory in the first five years if profits are not earned.

However, the critical law which inhibits worker association is that which declares the EPZs to be Public Utilities, under the Industrial Disputes Act, six weeks notice is required for a strike in a public utility service. Further, strikes are banned as long as any conciliation proceedings are pending. This makes the use of strikes as a bargaining weapon extremely difficult. It also means that labour laws can effectively be flouted without much resistance from the workers concerned. In any case, the predominant use of young women ensures that tendencies to unionisation are already low.

This is probably why it emerges clearly from virtually all the studies on EPZs [PRIA, 2000; Shah and Gandhi, 1998; Mazumdar 2000] that none of the provisions of the existing labour laws are actually met in most of the units operating in the major EPZs. Minimum wages are rarely if ever actually paid. (in Madras EPZ, women workers in leather and textile factories were reported to receive Rs. 800 per month in 1999, when the official minimum wage declared by the government at that time was Rs. 1200 per month.) Working hours are typically much longer than the specified maximum without any payment of overtime. The statutory benefits and leave rules are systematically flouted by employers. Basic safety and health precautions are also rarely observed within factories.

According to the PRIA study. Women do not get maternity leave anywhere, in fact women generally lose their jobs if they get pregnant. Surprisingly, some companies employ women on the condition that they won't get married or pregnant in near future. As per the factories law, employers are prohibited from allowing women to work in night shifts, but during the survey the contrary was seen women work in night shifts in many places in MEPZ. [PRIA 2000]

The questionable working conditions are obviously not confined to women workers alone, and it has been found that male workers in EPZs face very similar problems of low pay (typically lower than the official minimum wage) longer working hours and possibility of being fired without justification or compensation. The basic instrument through which all this is achieved is fear, the fear of loss of job as well as that of continuous harassment on the job.

This harassment, which ensures worker acquiescence, is often aided by the overt collusion of various agents of the government. Thus Mazumdar [2000], describes the state of affairs in the NOIDA EPZ: .even the tenuous rights available to workers ... are rendered further inoperable by a series of restrictions and practices by customs officials in the Zone. Designated a custom bound area, uniformed customs guards at the Gate screen all who enter the NEPZ, Passes are issued to each worker only at the behest of the management of companies. Similarly, they are immediately withdrawn and entry into the Zone is barred, again at management's behest. Illegally dismissed or victimised workers are thus prevented from even approaching the gates of their factories to lodge any protest. In other words, individual managements are able to use the uniformed customs guards as instruments of denial of workers rights. Even labour department officials cannot take workers who are illegally dismissed into the zone and there is no system of negotiation between the administrators of the zone and the labour department. Workers are deprived of the fundamental right to assembly. Gate meetings and demonstrations are totally banned in the zone. Although technically law and order fall in the purview of the UP Police, the Customs guards act as an extra-constitutional policing authority and have often displayed marked brutality towards workers. A police chowki is located inside the premises of the NEPZ and the factory managements, the zone administration and the police act in tandem to terrorise the workers.

The use of piece rate payment is another common instrument to ensure high rates of production at low rates of wages. Most studies have found that piece rate strategies of remuneration are increasingly being put into place in all manufacturing activity where this is feasible, and that this has put excessive pressure on workers. In some cases where the wage was not formally piece-rate production targets were arbitrarily increased without any increase in wages. Thus, in Noida EPZ, workers in garment factories found that their production targets had been increased from 300 to 600 pieces per workers per day without any additional labour saving device and certainly no increase in wages.

All the studies report a range of work-related illnesses and disorders, ranging from chronic headaches and stress-related fatigue, to back problems, to disturbances of the menstrual cycle, loss of weight and even more serious complaints. In all such cases, it was found that management had declared they were in no way responsible for the problems. As a result, dealing with such illness, with the associated absence from work and medical costs, was entirely the burden of the workers.

It is worth noting that these loopholes and strategies which allow for systematic labour exploitation in the EPZs have not made them more efficient or competitive than exporting units within the domestic tariff area which cannot avail of such benefits. Thus, as noted above, the share of EPZs in total value of exports has stagnated at the very low level of between 3 and 4 per cent, while that of Export-oriented Units (which get some fiscal and tariff incentives but no concessions in terms of labour laws) has tripled to around 11 per cent over the past decade. While employers of course maintain that the labour flexibility which is de facto provided in the operations of the EPZs is crucial in maintaining their profitability, this is questionable. In fact it could be suggested that such laws, by suppressing the cost of labour, actually promote more inefficiency in other aspects of the production process and discourage technological innovations which would enhance productivity.

MEASURES FOR SOCIAL PROTECTION OF WOMEN WORKERS

As most researchers in this area know only too well, it is easy enough to provide a catalogue of woes in terms of the working conditions and wages of women in export-oriented employment. It is much more difficult to work out policies and methods of ensuring some amount of work security and basic living conditions in the current global environment where the need to push for greater external competitiveness is systematically used as the basic argument against the provision of any workers rights.

In particular, the discussion above leads to certain fundamental questions which are extremely difficult to address. How is it possible to ensure a minimum provision of basic rights and privileges to women workers, and to improve the conditions of their work, without simultaneously eroding their attractiveness to employers and reducing the extent of female wage employment? How can such rights and basic labour standards be assured in the current phase of globalisation, in which heightened export competition is actually combined with a phase of aggregate manufacturing employment contraction, as the full force of the adjustment measures is felt in the real economies?

It is probably necessary to define the terms on which such social protection can be ensured. As pointed out by Huber and Stephens [2000], public delivery of a wide range of welfare state services is probably the most significant determinant of the conditions of the citizenry and of women in particular, and is much more significant than what are traditionally seen as straightforward redistributive transfers. Indeed, this argument has resonance in the Indian context, where many of the most basic of welfare state services are untouched by public agencies and expenditure on other has actually declined over the past decade as part of the standard structural adjustment-associated belt-tightening.

It is also true, as they suggest that there is strong political economy relationships associated with particular patterns of public spending as well as with the delivery of public services. This means that it would be foolhardy to specify certain social policies, without laying the groundwork for their adoption and efficacy through strong social movements which are able to demand these policies of the state. This is why it is necessary, in any discussion of social policy, to note the crucial significance of public pressure and social movements in achieving desired social outcomes, and therefore to realise why the ability to organise and the need to mobilise citizens is essential. Without this, even the most carefully thought out government policies and schemes are likely to have very different actual outcomes on the ground, with this caveat in mind, let us consider the basic requirements of worker protection in a country like India. The earlier discussion has made it clear that it is futile to expect either decent labouring conditions or viable standards of material income from private employers given the overall context of excess labour supply and low to stagnant employment generation. Thus, a significant share of the burden must necessarily fall upon the state, and it is necessary to generate sufficient social pressure to make the meeting of such requirements a basic political necessity for any government.

In India, it is clear that the dominant notions of how to proceed with the task of development have in turn influenced the measures for social security that have been undertaken by the government. [Gayathri 2001] Thus, in the period of the 1950s and 1960s, the need for welfare dominated policy thinking, leading to social security programmes along the lines of community development programmes and welfare institutions being set up for the most vulnerable groups. In the two decades subsequent to that is in the 1970s and 1980s the emphasis was on equality and equity. This led to the addition of programmes like the Integrated Rural development Programme which tried to provide basic assets to targeted rural beneficiary households, and the employment schemes under various titles. In the 1990s, when empowerment became the buzzword, there have also been measures such as reservation to political bodies, special financial assistance to vulnerable groups including widows, supplementary nutrition programmes for girls and pregnant and lactating mothers and more targeted schemes generally. As can be seen from this, there has been a related shift from ignoring the issue of social security (based on the earlier prevalent notions of the family or household as an altruistic unit) to one which recognises the need for gender-specific measures.

The most basic requirement for workers - indeed all citizens - in an economy like that of India is food security, that is access to sufficient basic food at prices which are compatible with the actual minimum household nominal incomes. This can and must be a priority of the state, which is why the implicit agenda of the current Indian government, of effectively dismantling the Public Distribution System for food (through inefficient targeting and higher prices) is so dangerous. Also, such a scheme should be universal in nature, which not only reduces administrative costs associated with targeting but also ensures that those who require it actually do have access. Quite apart from the general welfare considerations of such a strategy, it is well known that, given the social construction of gender in South Asia and intra-household consumption distribution, improved access to food for a household disproportionately benefits women and girl children, and the converse is true for reduced food access. [Ghosh 1998]

Similar requirements can be specified for public health programmes, which are not only grossly inadequate in India but are also dramatically under funded, and have experienced swinging cuts in expenditure over the last decade. As in curative health, preventive health measures and sanitation, which would be considered part of the most basic economic rights of citizens anywhere are also underprovided to an extent that would be unthinkable even in most other developing countries. The need to ensure adequate public provision of such health facilities is so obvious that it probably does not require restating. So also, public housing remains an important domain of development which can be crucially implemented by the state and its various agencies. [Mahendradev 2001].

Of course, the effectiveness of delivery systems in such public goods and services depends upon the degree of transparency and accountability that the system provides. This is why social experiments such as the move towards decentralised planning in the state of Kerala are so significant. [Isaac 2000] It is essential that local people and their elected representatives be given greater control not only in terms of choice of investments in these areas but also over the administration and delivery of such services.

All this being said, it should be noted that at least on paper, the intentions of the Government of India have been blameless - if singularly ineffective - in the past. There is a plethora of laws, as well as of specific schemes, which are designed to improve basic social security in these crucial areas. But mostly they do not have real operational strength, and this is because of a combination of poor and declining public funding and inadequate social participation and accountability.

This relates to the social security of citizens at large, but of course they affect women workers as well. But clearly, given the peculiar and potentially highly exploitative nature of employment in export manufacturing sectors, special measures need to be directed towards those in such employment, especially the more vulnerable category of young women. Once again, formally they are already covered by a range of announced interventions, as described in Table 1 below.

Table 1
Existing Models of Social Security in India

Model	*Nature of benefit*	*Beneficiaries*	*Admin/financial setup*
Employers liability	Workmens compensation Maternity benefit Gratuity Retrenchment compensation	Workers in the organised sector	Employers manage and pay exclusively
Social insurance I	Medical care Sickness benefit Maternity benefit Occupational injury	Workers in the organised sector	Administered by Employees. State Insurance Corp; financed out of contrib from employers, employees, state governments
Social insurance II	Old age benefit Invalidity benefit Survivors benefit Provident Fund	Workers in the organised sector and some workers in the unorganised sector	Administered by central board of trustees; financed out of contrib from employers, employees, state governments
Social assistance :			
(a) Welfare funds of central govt	Medical care Education Housing Water supply Old age benefit Survivors benefit	Mine workers Bidi workers Cine workers Construction workers	Administered by departments; financed by special levies in the form of cesses

Contd...

Model	*Nature of benefit*	*Beneficiaries*	*Admin/financial setup*
(b) Welfare funds of Kerala govt	Wide range of benefits including all of the above and housing, assistance for marriage, etc.	Workers in unorg sector such as handloom, coir, cashew production	Administered by autonomous boards; financed by contrib form employers, workers and others
(c) Subsidised insurance	Survivor.s benefit Invalidity benefit	Vulnerable groups of workers, incl handloom, agri, etc.	Administered by LIC and GIC; financed by contrib from state and central govts
(d) Other forms	Old age benefit Survivors benefit Maternity benefit Employment assistance Training, etc.	Persons outside job market and below poverty line, destitutes, orpahs, deserted and divorced women, widows, disabled persons, SC, STs OBCs	Administered by departments; financed from general revenues

References

Horton, Susan, (ed.), (1995), *Women and Industrialisation in Asia,* London: Routledge.

Wee, Vivienne (ed.) (1998), *Trade Liberalisation: Challenges and Opportunities for Women in Southeast Asia,* UNIFEM and ENGENDER, New York and Singapore.

Joekes, Susan (1999), A Gender-analytical Perspective on Trade and Sustainable Development, *Trade, Gender and Sustainable Development,* UNCTAD, Geneva.

Raman, R., Anant, (1989), *Review of Free trade Zones in Developing Countries,* Indian Institute of Foreign Trade, New Delhi.

PRIA (2000), Export Processing Zones in India and the Status of Labour, available at website *http.//www.pria.org.*

Mazumdar, Indrani (2000), Workers of the NOIDA Export Processing Zone, Mimeo, Centre for Women.s Development Studies, New Delhi.

Shah, Nandita and Nandita Gandhi (1998), Industrial Restructuring: Workers in Plastic Processing Industry, *Economic and Political Weekly,* Vol. XXXIV, No. 22, pp. L12-L29.

Huber, Evelyne and John D. Stephens (2000), Partisan Governance, Women's Employment, and the Social Democratic Service State, Mimeo.

Gayathri, V. (2001), Social Security for Women Workers, in S. Mahendradev *et al* (eds.) *Social and Economic Security in India,* New Delhi: Institute for Human Development.

Mahendradev, S. (2001), Social Security in India: Performance, Issues and Policies., in S. Mahendradev et al (eds.) *Social and Economic Security in India,* New Delhi, Institute for Human Development.

Isaac, T. M. Thomas, with Richard Franke (2000), *Local Democracy and Development: Peoples Campaign for Decentralised Planning in Kerala,* New Delhi, Leftword Books.

Micro Credit and Empowerment of Women Through Self Help Groups: An Insitutional Framework

A. ABDULRAHEEM* AND P. MUTHAIYEN**

INTRODUCTION

Micro-credit programs have been embraced around the world as an important strategy for poverty alleviation. Studies have demonstrated that poverty alleviation impacts of micro-credit services include reaching the poor, lifting their economic well-being, as well as empowering the poor, especially women. India has one of most extensive banking infrastructures in the world. However, millions of poor people in India do not have access to basic banking services like savings and credit. In the mid-1990s, about 70% of India's population lives in rural areas which account for only 30% of the bank deposits. About 70% of the rural poor do not have bank accounts and 87% of them do not have access to credit from banks. In the same period, the share of non-institutional agencies including traders, money lenders, friends and relatives in the outstanding cash dues of rural households was 36%. Therefore microfinance is considered as a useful remedy to eradicate poverty. Women form a vital part of the Indian Economy, who constitute one third of the labour resource, and primary member contributing in the survival of the family. It is true that women form the backbone of agriculture sector, comprising the majority of agricultural labourers in India.A significant development in recent years has been the mushrooming of community-based organizations

* Assistant Professor, Dept. of Economics, The New College, Chennai-14, (*e-mail: abdulraheem_amity@yahoo.co.in*)
** Reader, Dept. of Economics, Pondicherry University, Pondicherry.

and initiatives at the local level for women. Reports indicate that self-help programmes, often in the form of savings and credit or micro credit schemes, have succeeded in changing the lives of poor women, enhancing incomes and generating positive externalities such as increased self-esteem. This paper addresses the challenging issue of whether self-help micro credit programmes are tools for empowering poor women.

GROWTH OF MICROCREDIT : AN OVERVIEW

Microcredit is now accepted as a potential tool for poverty alleviation and socio-economic empowerment of the rural poor, particularly women in developing countries. There are many cases where it has proved to be a profitable business also for the microcredit institutions the world over. That it could be an ideal intervention at social, economic, financial and policy levels to address livelihood development issues has been agreed to at the World Microcredit summit which set a target of reaching 100 million of the world's poorest families (approximately 500 million people), especially the women of those families, with credit for self-employment and other financial and business services by the year 2005.

The goal of poverty alleviation through microcredit is particularly important to women. Women are found in the group of people who earn less than $1 a day. According to the Microcredit Summit women make up one billion of 1.5 billion people living in poverty. In Asia – pacific regions, over 900 million people in about 180 million households are poor earning less than one dollar a day. More than 670 million live in rural areas. In India, an estimated 260 million people live in poverty. After adjusting purchasing power of these poor who earns less than are dollar a day, about 39% of the Indian population comes under this poor people group. The World Microcredit Summit envisaged providing microcredit to 25 million poor families in India by year 2015. NABARD, the nodal agency for microcredit in India, set a target of credit linking 1 million SHGs in a decade's time that is by the year 2007 which has already been achieved, three years ahead of the schedule indicating that there is still a long way to go. Majority of the groups would be forming part of the SHG philosophy while some could come through alternate mechanisms comprising application of grameen model, credit unions and other emerging approaches. According to NABARD, 16.7 million people accessed microcredit during 2003-04 and the estimated number of people assisted up to March 2004 is 83.5 million which augurs well.

The cumulative number of SHGs financed by banks up to March 2004 is 10,79,091 and the number of poor families who have accessed bank credit up to march 2004 is 16.7 million. An estimated 83.5 million poor people were assisted till March 2004. About 90 per cent of the SHGs credit linked so far comprised only women members. Against the physical target of providing credit access to 25 million poor people by 2008, NABARD has reached 16.7 million people in 2004 and is likely to surpass the target by 2008. On the other hand, from the perspective of microcredit need for and ground level flow to the poor, the picture is entirely different. The estimated demand for and supply of microcredit to poor households by formal financial and social institutions reveals a massive supply gap. An estimated 75 million poor households live in India of which 60 million are rural households and 15 million are urban households. To provide credit @Rs. 2,000 per family, the annual credit requirement would be Rs. 120 billion. Another estimate for microcredit services excluding housing, is Rs. 500 billion assuming that average credit usage is Rs. 6,000/- per rural poor household and Rs. 9,000/- per urban poor household. Housing credit requirement is estimated at Rs.10 billion every year. Requirement in respect of saving and insurance services would widen the credit supply gap further. In India, a third of the population is below poverty line and majority of the people lack basic amenities. The most affected are the women and children. Women suffer from the unbearable burden of being women and being poor. A study found that only 0.2% of commercial lending reaches poor women. A study of 38 branches of major banks in India found that only 11% of the borrowers are women.

NEXUS OF MICRO CREDIT AND WOMEN EMPOWERMENT

The micro credit that is popular at present is not new. The micro credit and lending had been in practice since man started trade. The micro credit, which is claimed to be contributing to women through SHGs, was in existence prior to it in the name of SGSY, SGSRY etc. In all these programmes finance has been the central focus. They play a significant role in transferring funds from surplus to deficit sectors but hardly the formal banks concentrate on rural poor borrower particularly in backward areas. In all these processes of development of financial institutions, continued to be marginalized and lack all center to credit. Given this background it was felt by the women's associations and other organizations, that there is a need to mainstreaming of women so that the human resource development would be complete, the economic development would be better with the contribution of the other half of the human resource and also the gender disparity will be addressed. However, till the 1970s no organized efforts were made to mainstream the women by extending equal opportunities in education, nutrition and health. It is believed and established theoretically that economic independence of women would empower and mainstream the women. However, there are others who argue that economic empowerment alone will not contribute completely to women's empowerment rather economic empowerment along with social empowerment is necessary so that mainstreaming of women is possible.

Realizing these needs, government of India has implemented several schemes of assistance since the 1970s in the name of development and poverty alleviation programmes. and the Entrepreneurship Development Programmes for Women by various agencies including District Industries Centre, Industrial Promotional Agencies etc., which were able to extend some micro credit assistance in rural areas. Under these schemes the SHGs are encouraged. It is since 1975, the United Nation's declarations of Women Empowerment Decade, every effort towards ensuring gender equality was recognized everywhere. Several approaches have been followed to empower women and address the gender disparities in the society. In the beginning in India the efforts taken to support women were related to welfare programmes in which the women were treated as beneficiaries. Later equity approach was followed in which women were facilitated to be equal citizens in the field of economic participation. Later the equity approach was replaced by empowerment approach, which emphasized that the women must be given equal power and must come to the mainstream to prove their capabilities.

The concept of empowerment has been the subject of much intellectual discourse and analysis. Empowerment is defined "as the processes by which women take control and ownership of their lives through expansion of their choices". The core elements of empowerment have been defined as agency (the ability to define one's goals and act upon them), awareness of gendered power structures, self-esteem and self-confidence. The micro financing schemes in India came with the introduction of SHG concept by NABARD for the first time in the government sector. In the non-government level, Self-Employment Association of Women [SEWA] founded by Ela Bhatt was the first of it kind as Grameen Bank in Bangladesh. Later on several other organizations such as RASS, SHARE in Hyderabad, MYRADA in Karnataka and WWF in Chennai and various organizations in various parts of Southern India proved to be very successful in empowering women economically through the micro credit programmes. NABARD a bank for rural development has conceived the concept of SHGs with full support and vigor and succeeded in establishing that Self-Help is the best help to progress. There are three approaches emerged in the SHG concept.

- NGOs facilitated SHGs in which the NGOs would be helping the members to form the group and arrange to get the support from financial agencies directly just playing a facilitator's role.
- NGO intermediated in which not only the NGO would form and organize the groups but also extend credit directly to members either getting from banks or other promotional agencies.
- Directly formed SHGs, which are formed by the banks and credit, extended directly to them without any facilitating or intermediating agencies. It is necessary to find out which of these approaches would be sustainable so that the contribution of SHGs in the initial years would continue to exist throughout the period.

It was revealed in a survey conducted by NABARD (1994) that micro finance can be a powerful instrument initiating a cyclical process of growth and development.

MICROCREDIT THROUGH SHG: AN INSTITUTIONAL FRAMEWORK

NABARD

The experiences of these early efforts led to the approval of a pilot project by NABARD in 1992. The pilot project was designed as a partnership model between three agencies, viz., the SHGs, Banks and NGOs. Initially there was a slow progress in the programme up to 1999 as only 32,995 groups were credit linked during the period 1992 to 1999. Since then the programme has been growing rapidly and the number of SHGs financed increased from 81,780 in 1999-2000 to more than 6.20 lakh in 2005-06 and 6.87 lakh in 2006-07.

Loan Repayments: One of the distinctive features of the SHG - Bank Linkage Programme has been very high on-time recovery. As on June 2005, the on-time recovery under SHG - Bank Linkage Programme was 90% in commercial banks, 87% in RRBs and 86% in cooperative banks.

Group Loans to SHGs and SHG Loans to Members: The average loan provided to SHGs by the banks for the last three years is presented in the following Table 1.

Table 1
Loan Provided to SHGs by the Banks

	No. of SHGs financed		*Bank Loan Rs in Crore*		*Per Group Loan (Rs.)*	
Year	*New*	*Existing*	*New*	*Existing*	*New*	*Existing*
2006-07	361731	171669	1157.74	697.74	32005	40644
2007-08	539365	258092	1726.60	1267.60	32012	49114
2008-09	620109	344502	2330.45	2168.63	37581	62949

Source: Computed.

NABARD shall play a pro-active role and identify new initiatives that will contribute to effectively improving outreach to the poor thru' SHGs, MFIs, etc.

Commercial Banks

A commercial bank is a type of financial intermediary and a type of bank. Commercial banking is also known as business banking. It is a bank that provides checking accounts, savings accounts, and money market accounts and that accepts time deposits.

Syndicate Bank

Syndicate Bank was established in 1925 in Udupi, the abode of Lord Krishna in coastal Karnataka with a capital of Rs. 8000/- by three visionaries - Sri Upendra Ananth Pai, a businessman, Sri Vaman Kudva, an engineer and Dr. T M A Pai, a physician - who shared a strong commitment to social welfare. Their objective was primarily to extend financial assistance to the local weavers who were crippled by a crisis in the handloom industry through mobilising small savings from the community.

Priority for Women - Towards Greater Empowerment: Women have occupied pride of place in the Bank in employment as well as in credit dispensation. Out of 1.16 lac Self Help Groups with credit assistance of Rs. 812 crore financed by the Bank up to 31.03.2008, 0.94 lac groups with credit assistance amounting Rs. 647 crore are for women groups. Women groups constitute more than 81% in terms of number and 78% in terms of amount. Out of total 2.48 lac unemployed youth trained for taking up self-employment ventures at Syndicate Institute of Rural Entrepreneurship Development (SIRD) and RUDSETIs sponsored by the Bank, 0.91 lac constituting 36% were women candidates.

United Bank of India

United Bank of India (UBI) is one of the 14 major banks which were nationalized on July 19, 1969. Its predecessor the United Bank of India

Ltd., was formed in 1950 with the amalgamation of four banks viz. Comilla Banking Corporation Ltd. (1914), Bengal Central Bank Ltd. (1918), Comilla Union Bank Ltd. (1922) and Hooghly Bank Ltd. (1932) (which were established in the years indicated in brackets after the names).

Table 2
Term Loan and Rate of Interest

Slab	Revised w.e.f 01.04.2009
Limit up to Rs. 50000/-	BPLR – 3.50% i.e.8.75%
Limit over Rs. 50000/-and upto Rs. 200000/-	BPLR – 2% i.e.10.25%
Limit over Rs. 200000/-and up to Rs. 500000/-	BPLR – 0.75% i.e.11.50%
Limit over Rs. 500000/-and up to Rs. 1000000/-	BPLR + 0.25% i.e.12.50%
Limit over Rs. 1000000/-	As per Credit Risk rating (Min 10.75% Max 14.25%

Source: Computed.

State Bank of India

The Bank is actively involved since 1973 in non-profit activity called Community Services Banking. All our branches and administrative offices throughout the country sponsor and participate in large number of welfare activities and social causes. Our business is more than banking because we touch the lives of people anywhere in many ways. Our commitment to nation-building is complete & comprehensive. SBI has taken up SHG movement as a mission. A noble mission to reach those families who were hitherto having no access to the credit by any formal financial institution and, therefore, were depending on informal sources and moneylenders.

Table 3
Credit Limit and Repayment

Size of credit limit	*Repayable up to 3 years*	*Repayable in 3 years and above*
Upton Rs. 50,000/-	8.5 %	9 %
Over Rs. 50,000/- up to Rs. 2 lacs	9.5 %	9.75 %
Over Rs. 2 lacs up to Rs. 5 lacs	10.25 %	10.25 %
Over Rs. 5 lacs up to Rs. 25 lacs	11.25 %	11.75 %
Over Rs. 25 lacs based on credit risk assessment	10.75 % to 12.25 %	11.25 % to 12.75 %

Source: Computed.

Micro finance is not new to State Bank of India. Bank's association with non-government organizations (NGOs) or voluntary agencies in extending financial help can be traced as far back as 1976 well before NABARD introduced SHG-Bank Credit Linkage Programme as a pilot project in 1992.

Steady Growth of SHG-Bank Credit Linkage Programme: SBI has actively participated in SHG-Bank Credit Linkage programme since its inception in 1992 as a pilot project of NABARD. Since then the Bank has made a steady progress in financing SHGs. As on March 2006, SBI's branches spread throughout the length and breadth of the country have opened 6,30,067 Savings Bank account of SHGs out of which more than 5.41 lacs SHGs have been provided with credit facilities thus benefiting more than 75 lacs poor people. Majority of these SHGs are women SHGs. The year-wise cumulative position of SHGs-Bank Linkage programme for the last 4 years is as under.

Table 4
Cumulative Position of SHGs-Bank Linkage Programme

Year	*March '04*	*March '05*	*March '07*	*March '08*
SHGs linked (financed)	1,07,553	1,74,666	3,43,691	5,40,481
No. of beneficiaries	12,33,660	21,50,752	48,11,674	75,68,842
Amount disbursed	324.84 cr.	614.87 cr.	1311.45 cr.	2262.95 cr.
Amount outstanding	269.43 cr.	462.77 cr.	872.08 cr.	1459.89 cr.
No. of SHGs maintaining Savings a/c in the Bank	2,79,466	3,69,568	5,08,396	6,36,067
Amount in Savings a/c (Amt. in Rs.)	261.36 cr.	348.31 cr.	411.82 cr.	434.07 cr

Source: Computed.

Non Government Agencies

"NGOs or NGDOs are basically voluntary organizations other than cooperatives, Self-Help Groups (SHGs) etc. Voluntary organizations, known for their virtues of human touch, dedication, great initiatives, self-reliance, contextual innovations, flexibility, togetherness with community and ability to reach the masses in the most effective manner are now considered partners of government in its all endeavors concerning needy, poor, children and women and their environment. Of late, it has been noticed that some NGOs are proving to be self-centered instead of mass-centered which these ought to be. The present compilation discusses some pertinent issues highlighting NGOs in India, e.g. emergence, growth, role and performance appraisal. Undoubtedly, this will serve as good reference tool to all concerned." (Jacket).

Other Institutions and Schemes

National Schedule Caste Finance and Development Corporation

Micro-credit Finance Scheme

(i) UNITCOST: NSFDC provides Micro Credit Finance for units costing up to Rs. 30,000/-

(ii) QUANTUM OF ASSISTANCE : NSFDC provides loans up to Rs. 90% of the Project Cost. However, under the Central-Sector Scheme of Special Central Assistance to the Scheduled Castes Sub Plans, the Below Poverty Line (BPL) Beneficiaries are eligible for subsidy @ Rs. 10,000/- or 50% of the unit cost, whichever is less. Wherever the Beneficiaries are not provided subsidy, the SCAs shall provide their share of Margin Money.

(iii) INTEREST RATES: The NSFDC shall charge interest @ 2% p.a. from the SCAs, which in turn, shall charge 5% p.a. from the Beneficiaries.

(iv) REPAYMENT PERIOD: Loan under Micro-Credit Finance is to be repaid in quarterly-installments within a maximum period of three years from the date of each Disbursement, including the moratorium period of 90 days for fund utilization.

(v) On repayment of loans under Micro-Credit, through the concerned SCAs, the eligible beneficiaries can avail any loan under NSFDC scheme.

Donbosco Anbuillam Social Service Society

This society committed to social justice, sustainable development and human rights. The right to communicate freely is a basic human right and a necessity for sustainable development. Access to information is essential to informed decision-making at all levels.

This society is committed to the dissemination of information and promotion of sustainable development initiatives, in response to the needs of underrepresented and marginalized sectors of society. For bridging the data gap and improving information availability we are committed to develop and establish an ideal medium for the Participation and exchange of a trusted and accurate source of quality information.

Tamilnadu Corporation for Development of Women Ltd.

To build capacity of poor and disadvantaged women in order that they are enabled to cross all social and economic barriers, and thereby facilitate their full development into empowered citizens;

- To reach out to 35 lakh BPL families in TamilNadu with focus on SC/ST, widows, physically handicapped and destitute for social, economic and political empowerment.
- To achieve the equality of status of poor women as participants, decision makers and beneficiaries in the democratic, economic, social and cultural spheres of life;
- To create or reorient democratic, economic and social processes and institutions to enable poor women to participate fully and actively in decision-making in the family and community, and at the local, district, state and national levels;
- To empower women to work together with men as equal partners and to inspire a new generation of women and men to work together for equality, sustainable development, and communal harmony;
- To promote and ensure the human rights of women at all stages of their life cycle.
- To advocate changes in government policies and programmes in favor of disadvantaged women.

The SHG movement with nearly 59 lakh women as members has grown from strength to strength over the years bringing about substantial social change. It would be the endeavor of the Corporation to extend the benefits of the SHG approach to the uncovered areas of the state and uncovered sections of society. The immediate goal of TNCDW is to ensure that all poor women particularly widows, destitute and marginalized are included in SHGs in the next three years. TNCDW has been very successful in bringing about social empowerment of women which has not fully translated into economic empowerment. The Corporation will strive to promote more economic activities among SHG women by converging Mahalir Thittam and SGSY implementation.

Swarnjanti Gram Swarozgar Yojana (SGSY)

Programme for self-employment of the poor has been an important component of the anti-Poverty programmes implemented through government initiatives in the rural areas in India. The Swarnjayanti Gram Swarozgar Yojana (SGSY) is the major on-going programme for the self-employment of rural poor at present. The basic objective of the SGSY is to bring the assisted poor families (Swarozgaris) above the Poverty Line by providing them income-generating assets through a mix of bank credit and governmental subsidy. The programme aims at establishing a large number of micro enterprises in rural areas based on the ability of the poor and potential of each area. The SGSY is different from earlier Programmes, in terms of the strategy envisaged for its, implementation. It has been conceived as a holistic Programme of self-employment. It covers all aspects of self-employment of the rural poor viz. organization of the poor in to Self Help Groups (SHGs) and their capacity building, training, selection of key activities, planning of activity clusters, infrastructure build up, technology and marketing support.

Swarna Jayanti Shahari Rojgar Yojana (SGSRY)

The Swarna Jayanti Shahari Rojgar Yojana (SJSRY) is a unified Centrally Sponsored Scheme launched a fresh in lieu of the erstwhile Urban Poverty Alleviation Programmes viz., Nehru Rojgar Yojana (NRY), Prime Minister's Integrated Urban Poverty Eradication Programme (PMIUPEP) and Urban Basic Services for the Poor (UBSP).

- Gainful Employment to Urban Poor, Unemployed and Underemployed.
- Setting up self Employment ventures and provision of wage-employment.
- Community Empowerment through creation of suitable community structures on UBSP pattern.
- Capability Building, Women's Group for small enterprises, Women's Thrift-cum-Credit Societies.

Development of Women and Children in Urban Areas (DWCUA)

This Scheme is distinguished by the special incentive extended to urban poor women who decide to set up self employment ventures in a group as opposed to individual effect. Group of urban poor women shall take up an economic activity suited to their skill, training, aptitude, and local conditions.

CONCLUSION

The microfinance in India is turning into a profitable as well as a socially responsible affair slowly. The government of India is also encouraging the participation of domestic and foreign institutions to enter into the microfinance sector. The participation of more and more financial institution and foreign investment implies more funds for lending to the poor people, ultimately which will result into the poverty eradication and economic balance in the country. Perhaps this is the first time in India that the microfinance which primarily focuses on the economic development of the poor, promising a thick amount of profit for capitalists also. However, the main aim of microfinance should always be the betterment of the poor class of people. No doubt the microfinance sector in India is going towards commercialization in order to earn maximum profit, which is the ultimate aim of every business firm, but this great revolution should not deviate from its motto. Ultimately we can conclude that a new era has already been started in the Indian microfinance sector which will help India to eradicate the poverty. Micro finance is a movement and an institution, which has reached its heights in every parts of the country. It is popularized as a right strategy to address the poverty among poor nations. UN declared year 2005 as the international year of micro financing. It has significance as the micro credit summit is reaching its final year by 2008. The empowerment of the stakeholders of SHG has been revealed that both social and economic empowerment were realized by the SHG but the social empowerment in terms of involvement in community activities, participation in community development and decision making affairs of family and society and other related aspects were more than economic empowerment in terms of incremental income, asset value, increase in consumption expenditure, change in consumption pattern, increase in savings, thrift, etc are minimal. Hence there is need for more economic empowerment, which would take care of other aspects.

References

Cheston, Susy and Lisa Kuhn (2002), "Empowering Women Through Microfinance", unpublished Background Paper for the Microcredit Summit + 5, New York, 10-13 November.

ESCAP (2002), *Social Safety Nets for Women,* forthcoming United Nations Publication.

Food and Agriculture Organization of the United Nations (2002), "Gender Responsive Echnology for Poverty Alleviation", Unpublished Draft Report.

Goetz, A. and R. Sen Gupta (1996), "Who Takes the Credit? Gender, Power and Control Over Loan Use in Rural Credit Programmes in Bangladesh", *World Development,* Vol. 24, No. 1.

Kabeer, N. (2001), "Resources, Agency, Achievements: Reflections on the Measurement of Women's Empowerment", in *Discussing Women's Empowerment–Theory and Practice,* SIDA Studies No. 3.

Krishnaraj, Maithreyi and Thelma Kay (2002), "Report of Review of IFAD Gender Mainstreaming Projects in Asia", Unpublished Paper Prepared for IFAD.

Lalitha, N. and B. S. Nagarajan (2002), *Self-Help Groups in Rural Development* (New Delhi, Dominant Publishers and Distributors).

Putnam, R. (2000), *Bowling Alone: The Collapse and Revival of American Community,* (New York, Simon & Schuster).

Simanowitz, Anton and Alice Walker (2002), "Ensuring Impact: Reaching the Poorest while Building Financially Self Sufficient Institutions, and Showing Improvement in the Lives of the Poorest Women and their Families", Unpublished Background Paper for the Microcredit Summit + 5, New York, 10-13 November.

United Nations (2001), "Empowerment of Women Throughout the Life Cycle as a Transformative Strategy for Poverty Eradication" (EGM/POV/2001/REPORT).

United Nations Development Programme (1997), "Sustaining Livelihoods: Promoting Informal Sector Growth in Pacific Island Countries", Unpublished Paper. , 1999.

"Report on Microfinance and HIV/AIDS Workshop", Malaysia (2001), "Participatory Governance, People's Empowerment and Poverty Reduction", UNDP Conference Paper Series.

World Bank (1998), *PREMnotes*, No. 8 (Washington, World Bank).

Yunus, Muhammad, with Alan Jolis (1998), *Banker to the Poor: The Autobiography of Muhammad Yunus* (London, Aurum Press).

Yunus, Muhammad (2002), "Grameen Bank II: Designed to Open New Possibilities", 8 November 2002.

Zaman, H. (2001), "Assessing the Poverty and Vulnerability Impact of Micro-Credit in Bangladesh: A Case Study of BRAC", Unpublished Background Paper for World Bank, *World Development Report 2000/2001* (Washington, World Bank).

Present Status of Commodity Derivative Market in India: Regulation and Policy Issues

K. SAMBASIVAM* AND A. ABDULRAHEEM**

INTRODUCTION

Derivatives markets have been in existence in India in some form or other for a long time. In the area of commodities, the Bombay Cotton Trade Association started futures trading in 1875 and, by the early 1900s India had one of the world's largest futures industries. In 1952 the government banned cash settlement and options trading and derivatives trading shifted to informal forwards markets. In recent years, government policy has changed, allowing for an increased role for market-based pricing and less suspicion of derivatives trading. The ban on futures trading of many commodities was lifted starting in the early 2000s, and national electronic commodity exchanges were created.

In the equity markets, a system of trading called "badla" involving some elements of forwards trading had been in existence for decades.6 However, the system led to a number of undesirable practices and it was prohibited off and on till the Securities and Derivatives Exchange Board of India (SEBI) banned it for good in 2001. A series of reforms of the stock market between 1993 and 1996 paved the way for the development of exchange-traded equity derivatives markets in India. In 1993, the government created the NSE in collaboration with state-owned financial institutions. NSE improved the efficiency and transparency of the stock markets by offering a fully automated screen-based trading system and real-time price dissemination. In 1995,

* Associate Professor, Dept. of Economics, Bharathidhasan Govt. Arts College for Women, Pondy-3, (*e-mail: sambasivam2009@gmail.com*)

** Assistant Professor, Dept. of Economics, The New College, Chennai-14, (*e-mail: abdulraheem_amity@yahoo.co.in*) a prohibition on trading options was lifted. In 1996, the NSE sent a proposal to SEBI for listing exchange-traded derivatives. The report of the L. C. Gupta Committee, set up by SEBI, recommended a phased introduction of derivative products, and bi-level regulation (i.e., self-regulation by exchanges with SEBI providing a supervisory and advisory role). Another report, by the J. R. Varma Committee in 1998, worked out various operational details such as the margining systems. In 1999, the Securities Contracts (Regulation) Act of 1956, or SC(R)A, was amended so that derivatives could be declared "securities." This allowed the regulatory framework for trading securities to be extended to derivatives. The Act considers derivatives to be legal and valid, but only if they are traded on exchanges. Finally, a 30-year ban on forward trading was also lifted in 1999.

The economic liberalization of the early nineties facilitated the introduction of derivatives based on interest rates and foreign exchange. A system of market-determined exchange rates was adopted by India in March 1993. In August 1994, the rupee was made fully convertible on current account. These reforms allowed increased integration between domestic and international markets, and created a need to manage currency risk. Figure 1 shows how the volatility of the exchange rate between the Indian Rupee and the U.S. dollar has increased since 1991. The easing of various restrictions on the free movement of interest rates resulted in the need to manage interest rate risk.

DERIVATIVES USERS IN INDIA

The use of derivatives varies by type of institution. Financial institutions, such as banks, have assets and liabilities of different maturities and in different currencies, and are exposed to different risks of default from their borrowers. Thus, they are likely to use derivatives on interest rates and currencies, and derivatives to manage credit risk. Non-financial institutions are regulated differently from financial institutions, and this affects their incentives to use derivatives. Indian insurance regulators, for example, are yet to issue guidelines relating to the use of derivatives by insurance companies.

In India, financial institutions have not been heavy users of exchange-traded derivatives so far, with their contribution to total value of NSE trades being less than 8% in October 2005. However, market insiders feel that this may be changing, as indicated by the growing share of index derivatives (which are used more by institutions than by retail investors). In contrast to the exchange-traded markets, domestic financial institutions and mutual funds have shown great interest in OTC fixed income instruments. Transactions between banks dominate the market for interest rate derivatives, while state-owned banks remain a small presence. Corporations are active in the currency forwards and swaps markets, buying these instruments from banks.

Why do institutions not participate to a greater extent in derivatives markets? Some institutions such as banks and mutual funds are only allowed to use derivatives to hedge their existing positions in the spot market, or to rebalance their existing portfolios. Since banks have little exposure to equity markets due to banking regulations, they have little incentive to trade equity derivatives. Foreign investors must register as foreign institutional investors (FII) to trade exchange-traded derivatives, and be subject to position limits as specified by SEBI. Alternatively, they can incorporate locally as a broker-dealer. FIIs have a small but increasing presence in the equity derivatives markets. They have no incentive to trade interest rate derivatives since they have little investments in the domestic bond markets. It is possible that unregistered foreign investors and hedge funds trade indirectly, using a local proprietary trader as a front.

Retail investors (including small brokerages trading for themselves) are the major participants in equity derivatives, accounting for about 60% of turnover in October 2005, according to NSE. The success of single stock futures in India is unique, as this instrument has generally failed in most other countries. One reason for this success may be retail investors' prior familiarity with "badla" trades which shared some features of derivatives trading. Another reason may be the small size of the futures contracts, compared to similar contracts in other countries. Retail investors also dominate the markets for commodity derivatives, due in part to their long-standing expertise in trading in the "havala" or forwards markets.

EVOLUTION OF COMMODITY DERIVATIVE MARKETS

Commodity Derivative markets were set up in India in cotton in 1875 and in oilseeds in 1900 at Bombay. Forward trading in raw jute and jute goods started at Calcutta in 1912. Forward Markets in Wheat had been functioning at Hapur since 1913, and in bullion at Bombay, since 1920. In 1919, the government of Bombay passed Bombay Contract Control (War Provision) Act and set up the Cotton Contracts Board. With a view to restricting speculative activity in cotton market, the Government of Bombay issued an Ordinance in September 1939 prohibiting option business. Bombay Options in Cotton Prohibition Act, 1939, later replaced the Ordinance. In 1943, the Defence of India

Act was utilized on a large scale for the purpose of prohibiting forward trading in some commodities and regulating such trading in others on an all India basis. In the same year oilseeds forward contracts prohibition order was issued and forward contracts in oilseeds were banned. Similarly orders were issued banning forward trading in food-grains, spices, vegetable oils, sugar and cloth. These orders were retained with necessary modifications in the Essential Supplies Temporary Powers Act 1946, after the Defence of India Act had lapsed. With a view to evolving the unified systems of Bombay enacted the Bombay Forward Contract Control Act, 1947.

LEGAL FRAMEWORK

After Independence, the Constitution of India adopted by Parliament on 26 January, 1950 placed the subject of "Stock Exchanges and Futures Market" in the Union list and therefore the responsibility for regulation of forward contracts devolved on government of India. The Parliament passed the Forward Contracts (Regulation) Act, 1952, (FCRA) which presently regulates forward contracts in commodities all over India. Exchange controls were in place and RBI had jurisdiction over forex as well as money market. The Securities Contracts (Regulation) Act (SCRA) was enacted in 1957 on the lines of FCRA, 1952, but another department of the government regulated security markets. The Securities and Exchanges Board of India (SEBI) was given a statutory status in the year 1991. Derivative trading was introduced in securities as later as in the year 2001, after the term "security" in the SCRA was amended to include derivatives. Derivatives Markets in India: 2003 163 tracts in securities. Consequently, regulation of derivatives came within the purview of SEBI. We thus have separate regulatory authorities for forex, money market and commodity derivative markets. The experience has shown that the security market does not operate independently, i.e. without interaction with of money/forex market. The commodity derivatives market is relatively insignificant at present to be influenced by the money/forex markets. But this may not necessarily be the case in near future. In the USA, the Commodity Futures Trading Commission (CFTC) has jurisdiction to regulate all types of derivative contracts - forex, government securities, interest rates, equities etc. In U.K., even greater convergence of regulatory authority is achieved by vesting regulatory powers to a single agency, the Financial Services Authority, (FSA). In India, there have been occasions to disentangle of issues of regulatory jurisdiction between RBI and SEBI. The proposals of allowing stock brokers to trade in commodity derivatives market and regional stock exchanges being allowed to trade commodity futures contract are being discussed at regulatory levels. Therefore, similar issues of regulatory jurisdiction and the desirability of regulatory convergence are likely to become relevant. As issues involved have many more dimensions besides academic, and there is a will on the part of regulators to discuss issues with open mind, it would not be useful to take a particular position at this stage. As things stand, the Forward Markets Commission (FMC) continues to have jurisdiction over commodity forward contracts. The main features of the FCRA are as follows:

- The Act applies to goods, which are defined as any movable property other than security, currency and actionable claims.
- In the preamble of the Act itself, the intention of the legislature to prohibit options in goods is made explicit. By a specific provision, section 19, such agreements are prohibited. (The proposal to regulate options in goods is under consideration of the government.)
- The Act classifies contracts/agreements into two broad categories, viz., ready delivery contracts and forward contracts. Ready delivery contract are those where delivery of goods and full payment of price therefore is made within a period of eleven days. (The proposal to extend the period to thirty days is under consideration of Government). It is further clarified that notwithstanding the period of performance contract, if the contract is performed by payment of money difference (cash settlement), it would not be a ready delivery contract.
- The Act defines forward contract as the contract for delivery of goods which is not a ready delivery contract.
- Forward contracts are implicitly classified into two broad categories, viz., specific delivery contracts and non-specific delivery contracts or standardized contracts. Though, de-facto, the focus of the regulation are standardized contracts (futures contracts), these are not defined in the present Act (it is proposed to introduce definition of "futures contract" in the Act).
- Specific delivery contracts (where the terms of the contracts are specific to each contract – customized contracts) where the buyer does not transfer the contract by merely transferring document of title to the goods and exchanging money difference between the sale and purchase price (also termed as

Non-transferable Specific Delivery Contracts) are normally outside the purview of the Act. However, there is an enabling provision empowering the government to regulate or prohibit such contracts.

- The Act provides for either regulation of the other forward contract in specified commodities or prohibition of specified commodities. Such contracts in the commodities, which do not figure in, regulated or prohibited categories, are outside the purview of the Act, except when they are organized by some exchange.
- The Act envisages a three-tier regulation. The exchange which organizes forward trading in regulated commodities can prepare its own rules (articles of association) and byelaws and regulate trading on a day-to-day basis.

The FMC approves those rules and byelaws and provides regulatory oversight. It also acquires concurrent powers of regulation either while approving the rules and byelaws or by making such rules and byelaws under the delegated powers. The Central government - Department of Consumer Affairs, Ministry of Consumer Affairs, Food and Public Distribution - is the ultimate regulatory authority. Only those associations which are granted recognition by the government are allowed to organize forward trading in regulated commodities. Presently the recognition is commodity-specific. The government has original powers to suspend trading, call for information, require the exchanges to submit periodical returns, nominate directors on the Boards of the exchanges, supersede the Board of Directors of the exchange, etc.

Most of these powers are delegated to the FMC; otherwise the role of FMC is recommendatory in nature. The government has full control over the FMC, which is the subordinate office of the Department of Consumer Affairs, depending upon the budget allocation for its existence. The FMC also is subject to the rules and regulations relating to all matters including appointment of staff and officers, incurring office expenses and conducting tours, etc., as are applicable to any government Department.

- Only police authorities have powers to enforce illegal trading in prohibited commodities and options in goods.
- FMC can merely forward information and render technical assistance to police. The penalties provided under the Act are nominal and does not have deterrent effect. Since judicial

magistrate first class has jurisdiction to try offences under this Act, the fine cannot exceed Rs. 10,000.

- The minimum fine prescribed for the second offence is Rs.1,000 only. There is no provision to relate the penalty to the amount involved in the offence. (The government is considering amending the Act to raise the fine to Rs. 5,000).

PRESENT STATUS OF COMMODITY DERIVATIVE MARKET AND POLICY LIBERALISATION

Forward trading was banned in 1960's except for pepper, turmeric, castor seed and linseed. A future trading in castor seed and linseed was suspended in 1977. Apparently on the basis of the recommendations made by Khusro Committee, forward trading in potato and gur was allowed in early 1980's and in castorseed in 1985. After the process of liberalization of the economy started in 1990, the government set up a committee under the Chairmanship of Prof. K. N. Kabra in 1993 to examine the role of futures trading in the context of liberalization and globalization. The Kabra Committee recommended allowing futures trading in 17 commodity groups. It also 166 Regulation and Policy issues for. . . recommended strengthening of the FMC and amendments to the FCRA, 1952. The major amendments include allowing options in goods, increase in outer limit for delivery and payment from 11 days to 30 days for the contract to remain ready delivery contract and registration of brokers with the FMC. The government accepted most of these recommendations. Additional staff was provided to the FMC and the post of Chairman was upgraded to the legal of Additional Secretary to the government of India. The recommendations to set up Regional office at Lucknow, Delhi and Kochi were kept in abeyance for the time being. As of end 2002, futures trading had been permitted in all recommended commodities except bullion and basmati rice.

The commodity derivatives markets have gained some respectability with commencement of trading at National Board Board of Trade (NBOT, originally SOPA). Within two years of its operation, NBOT has been able to trade a significant fraction of the aggregate volume being traded by all the exchanges. The initial liquidity at NBOT was brought by the operators in the informal bullion market at Saraffa in Indore. Now the illegal trade in the Saraffa has vanished and the entire liquidity has migrated to the NBOT. The President of the NBOT facilitated the "pull and push" of these operators towards the legal market. The NBOT example shows that the leadership and channeling the liquidity from informal market to the official market was very significant in developing an exchange in a short run rather than the best systems and procedures and regulatory reforms. There is wide scope to replicate this model in mustard seed complex, kapas and bullion.

The other developments in the direction of further liberalization of commodity derivative markets are:

- In paragraph 44 of the National Agricultural Policy announced by the government in 1999, it was stated that the government would enlarge the coverage of futures market to minimize the wide fluctuations in commodity prices, as also for hedging their risk. It was mentioned that an endeavor would be to cover all-important agricultural products under futures trading in the course of time.
- An expert committee on agricultural marketing headed by Mr. Shankerlal Guru recommended linkage of spot and forward markets, introduction of electronic warehouse receipt system, inclusion of more and more commodities under futures trading and promotion of national system of warehouse receipt.
- A sub-group on forward and futures markets was formed under the chairmanship of Dr. Kalyan Raipuria (Economic Adviser, Department of Consumer Affairs) to examine the feasibility of implementing the recommendations made by the expert committee, which recommended that the commodity specific approach to the grant of recognition should be given up. Exchanges which meet the criteria to be stipulated by the Government, should be able to trade contracts in any permitted commodity.
- In the Budget speech made on 28 February 2002, the Finance Minister announced expansion of futures and forward trading to cover all agricultural commodities.
- The economic survey for the year 2000-2001 indicated the intention of the government to allow futures trading in Bullion.

The policy statements announced by the government indicate its resolve to introduce reforms in commodity sector. A number of initiatives were also taken to decontrol the spot markets in commodities. The number of commodities listed as essential commodities has been pruned down to 17.

CONCLUSION

To sum up, keeping in view the past baggage being carried by existing exchanges, the objective of catching up with the developed countries can be achieved in the short run by reviving the derivative markets by attracting traditional players. The policy liberalization in the physical and derivative commodity sector would help in reviving their interest. Simultaneously large-scale training programmes need to be launched for market participants who are not conversant with modern trade practices. The transition to the modern systems and practices need to be made by adopting policies which will unleash competitive pressures after the derivative markets are revived by traditional players rather than thrusting new systems and practices. Derivatives Markets in India: 2003 on the traditional players. For example, allowing the stockbrokers trading in derivative segment of the security markets to trade in commodity derivatives market would hasten the transition to modern methods of trading, clearing and settlement.

References

Chitale, Rajendra P. (2003), Use of Derivatives by India's Institutional Investors: Issues and Impediments, in Susan Thomas (ed.), *Derivatives Markets in India*, Tata McGraw-Hill Publishing Company Limited, New Delhi, India.

Fitch Ratings (2004), Fixed Income Derivatives—A Survey of the Indian Market, *www.fitchratings.com www.fitchratings.com*

Gambhir, Neeraj and Manoj Goel (2003), Foreign Exchange Derivatives Market in India—Status and Prospects, Susan Thomas (ed.), *Derivatives Markets in India*, Tata McGraw-Hill Publishing Company Limited, New Delhi, India.

Gorham, Michael, Thomas, Susan and Ajay Shah (2005), India: The Crouching Tiger, Futures Industry.

Lee, Rupert (2004), Seeing Double, FOW.

ISMR, Indian Securities Market: A Review (2004), National Stock Exchange of India Limited, Mumbai, India.

Jogani, Ashok and Kshama Fernandes (2003), Arbitrage in India: Past, Present and Future, in Susan Thomas (ed.), *Derivatives Markets in India*, Tata McGraw-Hill Publishing Company Limited, New Delhi, India.

Nair, C. G. K. (2004), Commodity Futures Markets in India: Ready for, "Take Off"? National Stock Exchange of India Limited, Mumbai, India. Derivatives OUP 9.

Index

F

I

V

W

Z